The
Small
Meeting
Planner

The Small Meeting Planner

SECOND EDITION

by
Leslie E. This

Gulf Publishing Company
Book Division
Houston, London, Paris, Tokyo

The Small Meeting Planner

Library of Congress Catalog Card Number 78-72999

ISBN 0-87201-806-7

Building Blocks of Human Potential Series
Leonard Nadler, Series Editor

The Adult Learner: A Neglected Species,
by Malcolm Knowles
*The Adult Educator—A Handbook for Staff
Development,* by Harry G. Miller and John R. Verduin
Managing Cultural Differences,
by Philip R. Harris and Robert T. Moran
The Conference Book, by Leonard Nadler
and Zeace Nadler
The Client—Consultant Handbook,
by Chip R. Bell and Leonard Nadler
*Human Resource Development: The
European Approach,* by H. Eric Frank
Leadership Development for Public Service,
by Barry A. Passett
People, Evaluation, and Achievement,
by George Nixon
The NOW Employee, by David Nadler
Handbook of Creative Learning Exercises,
by Herbert Engel

Contents

Dedication

We learn from both failure and success. Encouragement and support comes swiftly from many when we do well. It is achingly lonesome and painful for the meeting planner after a mediocre meeting or one that fails. It is then that a "feller really needs a friend." This book is dedicated to the woman who always provided—in such moments—empathy, encouragement, solace and helped me to learn from poor planning when it was deserved . . . my wife, Delight.

Foreword

In the foreword to the first edition I noted that Les This and I had approached the topic of this book with caution. It was thought that perhaps the theme of the book was too "elementary" because many readers consider the science of planning and conducting a meeting as readily learned, while others consider it nonexistent.

There are those people who attend many meetings, few of which are successful. They tend to think that there is a magic about meetings and that some meetings simply work out well while others do not. There are other people who are concerned only with the practicalities of meetings; they deal with room size, cash bars, hotel/motel arrangements, etc.

Both of these groups are correct—in part. There is a certain amount of magic in bringing people together for a meeting. Professionals have found that even with the best of plans and controls, some meetings work, and some do not. We still have a great deal to discover about how to organize and conduct meetings to make them useful and beneficial.

Fortunately, a good deal of what is known appeared in the first edition of this book. It has now been supplemented by other material which adds to our knowledge and reduces some of the mystical aspects.

Since the original edition of this book, the field of conferences, conventions, and hallmark events has increased. There are new professional organizations as well as additional monthly publications. The field is growing and will continue to grow.

Those who wish to become more adept at planning meetings will find valuable help in this book.

Leonard Nadler
Series Editor

Preface

This book is not written for people who plan conventions or meetings for other very large groups. Rather, it is primarily intended for those who plan meetings, seminars, workshops, conferences and training activities for 100 or less participants. It can also be a valuable reference for those who are responsible for the individual sessions of a large assemblage.

Effective meetings are both a science and an art. The "art" aspect is difficult to explain and to teach. The "science" aspect is easier to grasp and is often seized upon as if it would assure the success of a meeting. There is a constant frantic search by meeting planners for the latest gimmick, piece of hardware or learning technique as if these would guarantee success. For example, discussion groups are still quite popular and have a strategic place in some kinds of meetings. But, as one disillusioned planner observed, "Nothing magical happens when you place people in a group. If you put six non-knowledgeable people together, all you get is compounded ignorance. There must exist in the individuals the knowledge and ability to solve the task assigned."

Simply reflecting upon the criticisms one hears about meetings indicates the basic problems: too many meetings; meetings too long; too much attempted; competition with other meetings; untrained and inept resource persons; those who should attend are not there; inadequate promotion; too limited and biased planning; objectives are not met; inadequate physical arrangements; little attention paid to operational timing; and holding meetings just because the calendar says it is time for one—"things worth talking about don't always occur on schedule."

This book primarily deals with the science side of meetings. It makes no claim to include all possible facets. It does attempt to include those factors and dynamics most often applicable and critical. The items may sometimes seem basic and elementary—but they are the ones most commonly violated. The book is also intended to serve as a "reminder list" and as a resource reference.

No book is as bad as it could have been; few are as good as they might have been. I had hoped to include other aids and resources for the meeting planner. Some desirable items could not be located; others were identified but reprint permission could not be secured; still others reluctantly had to be omitted because of book size limitations.

I would like to thank my wife, Delight, for her steadfast support and suggestions and for taking the major responsibility for raising our family while I was on the meeting circuit collecting experience and data. I am indebted to Dr. Gordon L. Lippitt for sharpening ideas in many critique sessions over the years. And certainly my sincere gratitude to all those meeting planners and participants who helped us learn—sometimes painfully—what did and did not make meetings effective and fun.

I gratefully acknowledge my appreciation to the following individuals and organizations for permission to use their articles and materials for illustrative purposes: Dr. Gordon L. Lippitt, professor of behavioral sciences, George Washington University; Dr. James Owens, professor of business administration, the University of Maryland; E. Leitz, Inc., Rockleigh, New Jersey; 3M Company, St. Paul, Minnesota; Adult Leadership magazine, Washington, D.C.; Fred I. Steele; BNA Films, Rockville, Maryland: American Heart Association, Inc., New York; The Presidents Association, Inc., New York; Scott Education Division, Scott Paper Company, Holyoke, Massachusetts; The League of Women Voters of the United States, Washington, D.C.; American Cancer Society, Inc., New York; North American Rockwell, El Segundo, California; and for the many related ideas found in the book Human Behavior, by Bernard Berelson and Gary A. Steiner, published by Harcourt, Brace and World.

The
Small
Meeting
Planner

Men must be taught
   as if you taught them not,
and things unknown
   proposed as things forgot.

Alexander Pope (1688-1744) Essay on Criticism

1
Roles of the
Meeting Planner

Before the individual meeting elements that must be woven into an effective mosaic are discussed, the role of the meeting planner should be examined. Dr. Gordon L. Lippitt has written an extremely insightful article on this subject*. It is reprinted herein.

While the article assumes that the meeting planner is internal to an organization, the planner who is not will have no difficulty in relating to the roles and to the functions. Often the meeting planner has more prosaic roles that he has to decide whether or not to play—presenter of content; meeting chairman; emptier of ashtrays; alcoholic beverages purchaser/purveyor; etc. For those who are consistently cast in these roles, it may be well to reflect on the objectives of their busy tasks.

*Gordon L. Lippitt, "Multiple Roles of the Meeting Planner," *Adult Leadership* 17, no. 4 (October 1968). Reprinted by permission of the publisher.

Business and industrial firms, government agencies, schools and other organizations in our society are placing more and more emphasis on creativity, innovation, and improvement in all kinds of meetings. It has been pointed out that there are 11 million internal meetings held daily by U.S. companies. It has also been established that 13,000 out-of-office meetings were staged in 1967. The cost of internal meetings is estimated at $1 billion annually, and out-of-office meetings, including conventions and trade shows, at $2.5 billion [1]. The pressure for improvement of all these meetings is producing an enlarging role and increased responsibility for skilled meeting planners.

This article attempts to examine the various roles a professional meeting planner is required to perform in meeting the complex needs of his organization, or one to which he is consultant. There are four major roles:

Role No. 1: As a Presentation Specialist
Role No. 2: As a Planner
Role No. 3: As an Information Coordinator
Role No. 4: As a Consultant to Management

It is my feeling that each of these functions requires somewhat different skills and abilities. In a small organization the meeting planner may perform all four functions, whereas in a larger organization the "head of a department" might well be the consultant to management for planning the meeting while those on his staff design, administer, and conduct the meeting.

It is probable that the roles of the meeting planner usually emerge in a sequence, as can be seen by reviewing the development of organizational meetings in this country. The earliest meetings were conducted by those who were more or less presentation specialists, recruited because of this particular skill to run sales meetings, new product sessions, or large conventions of organizations. As meetings grew in frequency and importance, the need for better planning became obvious. To insure the value of meetings, those who worked in business, industry, and government found themselves slowly moving towards the administrative role of planning. As a result, management, in selecting people to direct meetings, discovered it needed good administrators.

In recent years it has been felt that some meeting problems require for their solution a broader attack than that furnished by the usual

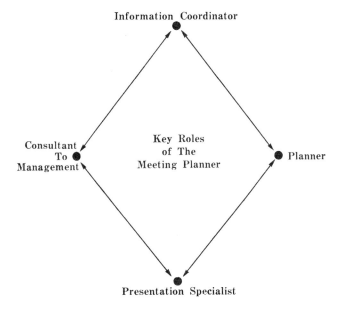

Figure 1.1. Multiple roles of the meeting planner.

meeting techniques. This brought into focus the need for the meeting planner also to be an information coordinator. The purpose here was to insure that meetings were planned on the basis of the communication goals of management. These goals encompassed the information needs of participants, adequate knowledge about the focus of the meeting, and effective information sharing prior to and at the meeting itself to insure confidence and trust in the meeting process.

At this point, the fourth role—that of contributing to organizational problem solving by being an internal consultant—has emerged.

It is quite likely that the roles of the meeting planner have emerged in this way within most organizations. The emergence of these roles does not mean, however, that the meeting planner has developed the skills necessary to meet the enlarging demands on his function and responsibilities.

Figure 1.1 illustrates the four roles which we will discuss. It is my feeling that every meeting planner should exercise the initiative to be professionally prepared in *all* four roles and functions.

As a Presentation Specialist

An important aspect here is that of the ability to use learning theory and effective presentation methods to meet the needs of a particular meeting.

People attending meetings will not be inspired, motivated, change, or "buy" an idea or produce unless they *learn* something from the experience.

In a recent paper about this need for sophistication about learning, it was stated as follows:

Since the [meeting planner] is concerned with learning, it follows that he should be concerned with learning theory. [Meeting planners] often talk about the learning theory that underlies their training. However, most of us do not have a good understanding of learning theories and their application to our training efforts [2].

The behavioral sciences in the last two decades have made major contributions in the area of learning theory, learning methods, and learning skills:

Research by the behavioral sciences in the learning process is also contributing to the successful practice of management. Recognizing that people come into a learning situation with an image of themselves as self-directing and responsible persons—not as dependent individuals—is one of the important realities to a superior trying to develop his subordinates. Also we know from behavioral science research that there are different levels of change in the development process. We know that people can increase their knowledge, insight, understanding, skills, attitudes, values, and interests; and we know that different methods are involved in developing different levels of these skills or knowledge [3].

The responsibility of an enlightened and effective meeting planner is to assure himself that one or more persons engaged in the planning process is knowledgeable in the field of learning principles and practices. This should be a prerequisite for effective meeting designs and, preferably, this knowledge should be held by the meeting planner himself. In addition, of course, he should be knowledgeable about the tools and methods of presentation to implement the goals of the meeting. This will include the direction of the program, coaching the presentors, selecting correct audio-visual equipment, securing proper facilities, and utilizing the best in human and technical resources. And it goes without saying that the meeting planner should always examine and improve his own presentation skills.

One of the great challenges to the meeting planning function, therefore, is the increased sophistication required in making use of the rapidly growing body of knowledge about how people learn and change, and relating this to the best of presentation methods and resources.

As a Planner

As organizational meetings have proliferated, the administrative role of planning has begun to demand a major portion of the meeting planner's time, skill, and energy. In this role he must apply all the administrative skills. He will need to recruit, select, and develop his staff team; plan programs; set up the process of coordination and communication; carry out financial planning for the meeting; and all of the other functions of a staff manager:

> The [meeting planner] should know the principles and practices used in the administration of programs. He should also know the concepts of management principles, including areas such as problem solving, the dynamics of organization, controls and reporting procedures [4].

But this requirement for managerial skills should not be frightening:

> There is nothing esoteric or mysterious about planning as such. It is simply a description of what we want to accomplish in the future and agreement on the means for achieving it. It is an effort to arrange for the use of our resources in an orderly, economical and goal-assuring way [5].

Dr. Lowell Hattery points out in his monograph, *Planning for Achieving Goals*, that these are the steps in the planning process:

1. Agreeing on and understanding the goals of the organization.
2. Gathering information on the nature of the current situation, prospective available resources, and future requirements (forecasting).
3. Involving others in the process.
4. Diagnosing needs and setting planning goals.
5. Choosing alternative courses of action.
6. Agreeing upon responsibility for action.
7. Preparing the final plan.
8. Getting the plan approved.

The planning function is increasing in importance within large organizational systems, and it is a critical area of skill for the sophisticated meeting planner.

As Information Coordinator

In this function the planner must serve as a seeker of information, clarifier of information, synthesizer of information, reality-tester of information, provider of information, and as a communications "link" in the organization.

Let us examine these functions in more detail.

As a *seeker* of information the meeting planner must discover the goals and expectations of his organization for the meeting to be planned. He must learn from those sponsoring the meeting what objectives and results are desired and who is to participate. He will want to request certain information from those who will guide the meeting from the platform. He will need to seek out information from those who know about the product to be presented, the program to be sold, the report to be achieved, and whether other input-output information is necessary so that the meeting can serve the proper function. This might be symbolized as follows:

As a *clarifier* of information the meeting planner will impart to the involved people, the multiplicity of ideas and information he has collected. A meeting in which there is no common understanding of intentions, plans and objectives is doomed to failure.

As a *synthesizer* of information the meeting planner will put into a proper frame of reference the different ideas and information which he obtains, bringing it all into focus so that the meeting is not a "hodge podge" of conflicting ideas and parts, but becomes an integrated meeting with a proper sequence of events around a basic theme.

As a *reality-tester* of information and communication, the meeting planner should always help his superiors, or sponsoring organization, to see that the plans they approve are feasible, workable, and realistic. The desires of management may not always be realistic in light of the allocated budget. The number of persons invited may not make possible the necessary learning goals; the facilities may not accommodate the necessary equipment. A professional meeting planner must assume responsibility for bringing reality into the planning process.

As a *provider* of information the meeting planner will give proper information and communication to those in the organization from his own experience. He should present ideas, opinions, and concepts that will be helpful in planning a successful meeting. If he cannot do this, he is a "functionnaire", and not a professional member of the management team.

As a *communications* link in the organization, the meeting planner is the pivot for management, departmental and technical personnel, the meeting presenter, and all others participating in the meeting. Obviously he must be an effective communicator. To be effective he will need to:

1. Be *accessible* to those who are working on the meeting; or who will participate in it;
2. Develop *trust* between himself and all others concerned;
3. *Level* with people on plans and problems;
4. Keep the *goals* clearly in mind, and help others to do the same;
5. *Define* the *responsibilities* of others;
6. Develop his *listening skills*.

In this way he will find this not only to be an essential role, but one which is seen as contributing to the greater assurance of a highly successful meeting.

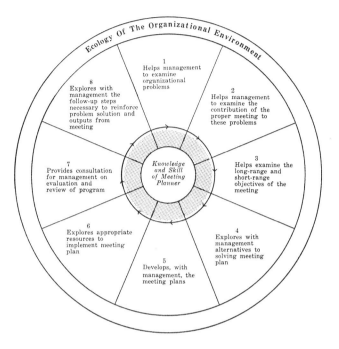

Figure 1.2. Problem solving function of the meeting planner.

As a Consultant to Management

I come now to the function the author feels is the most important one in the planner's portfolio—serving as a problem-solving consultant.

We have always recognized the need for management to support the meeting planner effort. It is not, however, the support of planning that is the major need. The major need is for meetings to be recognized and used as a valuable tool for management problem solving, which is itself a learning process. The meeting planning function should serve as an example and a resource to management in the solution of problems.

The new challenge for the meeting planner, then, is to develop his skills and roles in the organization as an internal organizational consultant on problem solving, change, and organizational development. Figure 1.2 illustrates the way in which this can be accomplished:

1. Helps management examine organizational problems (e.g.: organizes a management meeting for problem-identification in the relationships between home and field office personnel).
2. Helps management examine the contribution of the proper meeting to these problems (e.g.: in relation to home/field office problems, explores with management how a conference on communications might lead to problem solving).
3. Helps examine the long-range and short-range objectives of the meeting (e.g.: involves management in refining objectives and in setting goals).
4. Explores with management alternatives to meeting plans (e.g.: encourages the examination of the effect of different forms of participative type of meeting, as contrasted with solely a speaker or inspiration approach).
5. Develops, with management, the meeting plans (e.g.: based on the objectives, works with a steering committee to develop the program, rather than simply submitting an independently developed meeting plan for management for approval).
6. Explores appropriate resources to implement meeting plan (e.g.: provides management with a variety of resources, both inside and outside the organization. The meeting planner must help management to understand what each resource can contribute to effective problem solution).
7. Provides consultation for management on evaluation and review of program (e.g.: evaluation must be in terms of problem solving. Working with management, the meeting planner must make an assessment of the current status of the problem, rather than on whether or not the audience liked the meeting).
8. Explores with management the follow-up steps necessary to reinforce problem solving and outputs from the meeting (e.g.: encourages management to look at the implications of the steps so far taken, and to assess the current status of the problem in terms of other actions that might now be necessary to follow up on the stimulus of the meeting).

This "internal consultant" role of the meeting planner is important for the changing organizations of today's society. This role will require increased professionalization and skills in the meeting planner field.

In a sense everyone is a consultant. Everyone has impulses to give advice, information, or help. Teachers, parents, and friends are consultants. Also, everyone at times feels the need for help. In order that the consultantship between helper and the recipient optimally meets the needs of both parties, appropriate relationships must be built. It is necessary that both parties have certain kinds of skills, knowledge, and awareness in order to establish these relationships [6].

It is my feeling that more attention needs to be given by management to selecting and developing meeting planners who have the necessary skills. As Richard Beckhard puts it:

The consultant (or person in a helping role) always enters such a relationship as a person with authority achieved either through position or role in the organization or through the possession of specialized knowledge. To achieve an effective consultative relationship, it is essential that he understand the nature of this power and develop skills to use it in a way which will be viewed as helpful by the person receiving the help.

A person entering a consulting or helping relationship must have the ability to diagnose the problem and goals of the person being helped, and be able to assess realistically his own motivations for giving the help. He must also recognize the limits of his own resources to help in the particular situation [7].

In carrying out a "helping" relationship to management, a meeting planner will find himself operating along the continuum of consulting roles shown in Figure 1.3. Here I have illustrated some of the major helping relationships from directive to primarily non-directive consultations.

POSITION 1: Gives Expert Advice to Management

There will be numerous occasions when management will expect the meeting planner to answer a technical question; for example, a question about the value of a certain kind of meeting and its utilization for the organization.

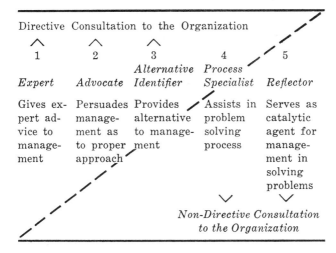

Figure 1.3. Multiple consulting approaches of the meeting planner.

POSITION 2: Persuades Management as to a Proper Approach

In certain circumstances management may be attempting to solve a problem by using a meeting medium or a method which the meeting planner, from his professional experience, feels will not work. The meeting planner may need to use his best persuasive skills, especially if time is short, to persuade management not to use that particular approach.

POSITION 3: Provides Alternatives to Management

The meeting planner may offer alternatives to management in the solution of a problem. The problem is not one in which he is the implementer of a solution, but one where he recognizes the values of identifying alternatives for management in confronting the learning aspect of a problem and the various kinds of meetings.

POSITION 4: Assists in Problem Solving Process

In this situation, the meeting planner serves as a process observer and consultant to management. He does not get involved in the "content" of the problem, which may be outside his area of competence. Rather, he helps management maintain the quality of its meeting and problem solving planning, through his skill as a specialist in this field.

POSITION 5: Serves as Catalyst for Management Problem Solving

In this last category, the meeting planner may only ask questions for management to take into account as it considers a certain direction, action, or meeting.

CHOICE FACTORS

The choice of which position to take at any given time as a consultant to management is conditioned by these factors:

A. Factors in the meeting planner as a person.
   1. Skills as a consultant.
   2. Ability to work with others.
   3. Experience in the area of the problem.
   4. Self-image.
   5. Level of knowledge and skill as a meeting specialist.
B. Factors in the relationship between management and the meeting planner.
   1. Status in the organization.
   2. Previous role in management problem solving.
   3. Familiarity with organization history and objectives.
   4. Ability to influence management.
   5. Previous successes and failures in working with other elements of the organization.
C. Factors in the problem situation.
   1. Knowledge of the content of the problem.
   2. Time available for solution.
   3. Ability to see alternatives.

The Challenge to the Meeting Planner

In this article, I have tried to present an inclusive view of the multiple roles of the meeting planner. With the greater demand for meetings, increased specialization of meeting designs, and the increased needs of organizations, I feel all these functions are needed. In many cases, management is not aware of the potential help it has available from its meeting planning, resource specialist. It should be said, however, that meeting planners sometimes have not been creative, innovative, or professional enough to see and fulfill all four roles and functions or to develop the skills necessary for their fulfillment.

This is a challenge to all of us who seek to meet the increasing demands placed on the meeting planner by today's organizations.

References

1. Bert Y. Auger, "How to Run an Effective Meeting," *Commerce* (October 1967).
2. Leslie E. This and Gordon L. Lippitt, "Learning Theories and Training," *Training and Development Journal*, reprint series (Washington, D.C.: Leadership Resources, Inc., April and May 1966).
3. Gordon L. Lippitt, "Implications of the Behavioral Sciences for Management," *Public Personnel Review* (July 1966).
4. This and Lippitt, "Learning Theories."
5. Lowell Hattery II, "Planning for Achieving Goals," *Monograph* (Washington, D.C.: Leadership Resources, Inc., 1966).
6. Jack R. Gibb, "The Role of the Consultant," *The Journal of Social Issue* 15, no. 2 (1959).
7. Richard Beckhard, *The Leader Looks at the Consultative Process* (Washington, D.C.: Leadership Resources, Inc., 1961).

Experience is a wonderful thing.
It enables you to recognize a mistake
when you make it again.

Anonymous

2
Basic Design Considerations

One of the basics in decision making is problem definition. As Alexander Pope once observed, "Too many people find the right answer. Too few know how to find, or ask, the right question." In defining a problem, it is cardinal to understand the total problem—sometimes called "situational familiarity."

Too often meeting planners do not understand the total context of a meeting, nor are they able to see the meeting as a process rather than an event. For example. many meetings are held not because they are really necessary, but because it is calendar time for the meeting or because the staff is being paid to say something on schedule. One problem with scheduled meetings is that things worth talking about do not necessarily happen on schedule. Often this is ignored; a meeting is indicated simply because in the course of organizational events it is time for certain people to say certain things.

14

Of all that is said in meetings, it would probably be appalling to determine why it is being said. Is it being said because those saying it really believe in what they are saying? Is it being said simply because it is expected or because someone is being paid to say his piece? As Marshall McLuhan has observed, when one has nothing to say, then form becomes important. Or, as another observer commented, when you have nothing to say, there is no point in saying it eloquently. Unfortunately, what usually happens is that the less one has to say, the more important become form, eloquence and theatricals. It seems as if one hopes the extravaganza will hide the void in content and significance.

What the meeting planner overlooks is that, as McLuhan has observed, the real message is too often the medium—participants rate the show and showmanship and overlook the message.

This is an age of remarkable technological advances. Every year something significant is expected to be discovered in the human relations and management area. Human behavior and management processes do not change as rapidly as technology. Yet, many organizations expect social scientists and management specialists to supply this year's latest findings, techniques and models. Not wishing to appear out of step with technological advances in the physical science arena, resource persons too often concur with the demand and substitute form, humor and psychedelic audiovisual aids for substance.

Many meetings fail because there is lack of planning, understanding of the meeting process, adequate preparation, flexibility to meet changing dimensions during the meeting or failure to comprehend the elements that must be integrated into the meeting process. Some mistakes will be beyond the control of the planner, as when the company president says he wants five minutes to welcome the participants and takes 90. This kind of failure, however, is usually infrequent. Planning lapses account for most ineffective meetings. The list in Figure 2.1 accounts for most of the elements in the meeting process. Most of them will be discussed, and their interrelationships will be shown.

Figure 2.1. Meeting process elements with which the meeting planner must concern himself.

1. A meeting is not an end in itself, it is on a continuum (something preceded the meeting, and something will follow it).
2. Who is coming? What are their needs and interests?
3. What are the meeting objectives? Can these be written out?
4. What is to be said?
   a. What is the theme of the total program?
   b. What is the purpose of each subpart of the program?
   c. How many objectives will be hit in each subpart?
   d. Is the subject matter immediately related to the meeting goals?
5. What kinds of program resource people are needed to meet the objectives?
6. What kinds of materials are needed?
7. What ways of presenting the material are best?
   a. Are the methods keyed to the nature of the subject and its place in the program?
   b. Can variety be provided to sustain interest?
8. What kinds of participation are desired?
9. What kinds of meeting aids are needed?
10. Can a physical facility adequate to accomplish the objectives be found?
11. How should the meeting be reported?
    a. As the meeting proceeds?
    b. At the end of the meeting?
    c. To whom should it be reported?
    d. Can the meeting remain flexible to meet unexpected needs as reflected by feedback?
12. Are any supplementary activities needed or wanted (for example, a cocktail party or field visit)?
13. How will the program be evaluated?
14. What kind of follow-up is desired?

Meeting Objectives

One of the first questions that confronts the meeting planner is, "Who will attend and what are the objectives?" Sometimes he will define who will attend and then look at objectives. Often who will attend is already decided, and he has little or no control over participant selection. Other times he will define the objectives and then determine who should attend. The two variables are closely interrelated.

There is a tendency to state the conference objectives in much too broad terms—"To save the world" is set as the objective when "How do I save Tom Jones?" is the real objective. The objectives for a given session might be as simple as to introduce participants to a new concept in motivation, to read five articles which will be distributed to participants or to have participants to look at this year's new model of a product.

In most organizational meetings the participants are known; the basic problem is that of setting objectives. Why are meetings held? The answers can be quite diverse as shown in Figure 2.2.

Figure 2.2. Reasons why meetings are generally held.

1. To protest against something
2. To promote something
3. To give out information
4. To solve a problem or make a decision
5. To organize for or against something
6. To exchange information or experiences
7. To find facts
8. To report to the members on something studied or on current status of an operation
9. To meet important persons
10. To initiate some specific action
11. For fellowship
12. For training in a skill, attitude or behavior
13. For inspiration
14. For no valid reason— it is simply time to hold a meeting.

Obviously, a meeting is not always needed to accomodate the reasons listed. If the objective is to give out information, it can be put in a book, company magazine, policy, directive, regulation, individually mailed record or tape, telephone, etc. The key issue for the meeting planner to answer is, "Why do I believe that a meeting is the best medium or vehicle to handle our objectives?" Once this question is adequately answered, half the battle of meeting design is won.

Too often the process of determining meeting objectives is oversimplified. One often finds a check list like the following:

1. Are the objectives clear?
2. Are they attainable?
3. Are they realistic in terms of time, audience and conditions?
4. Do they conflict or relate to organization policy?

These are valid questions and guidelines. However, objective setting is a complicated procedure. Generally, it is thought that the overriding consideration in objective setting is that of the attendants. Most often, this simply is not true. Who gets involved in setting the objectives for a meeting should be reflected upon for a moment.

The Participants. Often the participant's level of interest is an simple as "Where is the bathroom?"; "What time does the party start?"; and "Where's the night life?" Or, he has operational needs that are seen as too low level for consideration at the meeting.

The Chief Executive. Often his major concern is with visibility, that his people enjoy themselves and that his meeting pattern be in line with his industry or business.

The Chief Meeting Planner. His concern is that the registration exceed that of last year and that people "be happy."

The Board of Directors. "This group has got to get interested in legislation"–this is the concern of the Board of Directors.

The Planning Group. "Shall we have chicken or ham for the main banquet? This is the concern of the planning group.

The Prospective Member. "What's their angle? What's in it for me?" These are questions the prospective member asks himself.

The Training Director. "I'd like for the Training Department to look good and for some learning to occur," is what the training director might say.

The Resource Person. "Here's a chance to trot out my best speech, give it a title adapted to the one they want and hope I rate high so word will get around the circuit." This may be the concern of the resource person.

All objectives set for the meeting are a meld of these kinds of personal and individual considerations. To complicate the matter further, seldom do the participants speak with a common voice or agree upon what the meeting objectives should be. Sometimes there is real conflict in perception of the greatest need. The participants may feel they need help in closing sales; management may feel the most critical objective is to make them understand the latest financial procedures. Often a group that should be considered is voiceless—the customer or recipient of services. Seldom does anyone think to ask him what the group meeting could profitably discuss.

Determining Participants' Needs

A variety of techniques exist to help determine the training or meeting needs of the attendants. Elaborate research is not indicated. Often, if the operational people and meeting planners have been good listeners, they will have heard central themes coming from the prospective participants during the past year. Supervisors and managers have ideas, often valid, about what their people want and need.

A questionnaire can be sent to the participants. If the participant group is too large, it can be sent to a valid sampling. It may sometimes be filled in with little thought and may represent what they think they are expected to say. Although it often has little depth, it is much preferable to guesswork. It is useful to frame the questions so they can be tabulated. If it is simply framed, it normally ensures a better return. The questionnaire should be thought through in advance, keeping in mind the desired information to be secured. Representations that all responses will necessarily be reflected in the program should be avoided although the data will be considered. Open-ended questions are usually desirable, but they do make tabulation more difficult. On the other hand, open-ended questions often provide data that the questionnaire framers had not anticipated would be a crucial question or consideration.

A more desirable technique is that of individual interviews. The number needs to be sufficient to assure validity. One of its major advantages is that it permits the questioner to explain the intent of the question. Another advantage is that volunteered information and nonverbal communication may provide the most valuable guides and information. The interview allows for more depth, but the questioner's probing may suggest desired answers or introduce the element of bias. It is generally true that the more a person invests of his time and thought in a process, the higher is his expectation that his inputs will become implemented. For this reason, if a respondent's information cannot be included in the program, there is a greater risk that he will experience disappointment in the meeting. This can usually be handled by frankly discussing the purpose of the interview and the use that will be made of the data. The interviews can be either directive or nondirective.

A group interview may be a useful technique. One advantage is that you can reach more participants in a shorter time by fewer interviewers. It also has the advantage that participants can "piggyback" on the ideas of others—or get triggered onto a valid point by a contribution of another person. The process tends to reduce the amount of personal complaints, personal torches and irrelevant contributions. Sometimes the group can settle minor complaints and continue identifying more significant needs and issues. The interviews can be either directive or nondirective.

Other techniques include informal conversations, information from preregistration cards, review of complaints, interviews of customers or recipients of services, analysis of turnover, morale studies, review of problems, field reports and other performance and statistical data.

When getting data, the respondent should always be told

1. Why data is being collected,
2. What will be done with the data,
3. What usages will be made of the data at the meeting.

A technique that is receiving increasing usage is that of a problem census at the opening session of the meeting. This requires great flexibility by the meeting planners and the resource persons. Most often the group receives an overview of the agenda and program and is familiarized with the steps that led to its construction. They are then broken down into subgroups of five to seven persons to discuss the agenda to see if any critical items have been omitted or have arisen since the agenda was formalized. These are reported to the total group, and a decision is made whether critical identified items can be fitted into the existing agenda or program or whether the program should be modified. One technique often employed is to keep a time segment in the agenda open, or unplanned, to accommodate such items. A backup session filler should be ready to be inserted in this time block if the group does not identify an item they feel must be covered during the meeting.

Planning and Steering Committees

One of the most useful techniques to assist the meeting planner with the abundance of conflicting needs and perceptions of desired objectives is the appointment of a planning and steering committee. The group may go by a variety of names, but its functions are generally the same.

Insofar as possible, the committee should be composed of seven to nine persons. If more members are appointed, it ceases to be an operational committee and becomes a fact-finding committee or a conference itself. The members should include representatives who can fully reflect the needs and feelings of the intended participants, other major expectants of conference outcomes, one or two who are familiar with conference, training and meeting dynamics and design, one or two who are knowledgeable of the

Figure 2.3. Functions of the planning and steering committee.

1. Summarizing greatest needs and expectations, as they perceive them, of the major "conference expectants"
2. Crystalizing a set of objectives for the conference
3. Making suggestions as to who should attend
4. Serving as a communications link between the conference planners and the conference participants
5. Making recommendations about the conference design
6. Making recommendations as to the best time, place and dates for the meeting and other physical arrangements
7. Making recommendations as to needed conference organization
8. Meeting at appropriate times during the conference to assess how things are going, to provide feedback to the resource persons, to suggest desirable modifications or emphasis and to receive information they can help transmit to the participants.
9. Suggesting plans for evaluation and follow-up

subject matter to be dealt with at the conference and one or two who excel in creative ideas. Often more than one of these characteristics can be found in the same member.

Usually the planning and steering committee meets two or three times before the conference. Their functions are listed in Figure 2.3.

If it is at all possible, it is very useful to have the key conference resource persons and speakers attend one or more of the planning and steering committee meetings. It is a most helpful way to orient them fully to the objectives and purposes of the conference and to give them a "feel" of the conference dynamics.

The major traps to avoid in appointing and using such a committee are listed in Figure 2.4.

Figure 2.4. Traps to avoid in appointing a planning and steering committee.

1. Too many members on the committee
2. The committee confuses its role with that of the program planners and conference officers
3. The committee plans unrealistically
4. The committee does not know what they want to do and takes too long to make recommendations
5. The committee becomes a tight, cohesive group and alienates itself from the very organizational elements it was appointed to represent

The committee may also plan, if the conference is a recurring meeting, to have representation from this year's committee on the committee to be appointed for the following year's meeting. Meeting notes and working papers should be available to the planning and steering committee the following year.

Shall a Consultant Be Used?

Even in the organization of small meetings, the meeting planner, because of the strategic or critical nature of the meeting, will sometimes weigh the desirability of using a consultant to assist in the process of designing the meeting. A qualified consultant can be very useful under these conditions. How does one select a consultant? While his comments are not directly pointed to the small meeting planner, Dr. Gordon L. Lippitt has given some excellent guidelines in an article, "How to Identify a Professional Consultant."* The article is quoted in its entirety.

*Dr. Gordon L. Lippitt, "How to Identify a Professional Consultant," *Projector* (November 1969). Reprinted by permission of the publisher, BNA Films, BNA, Inc.

In this era of rapidly expanding institutions and organizations, we are finding an increased use of experts, consultants, specialists and resource persons of various sizes, shapes and forms. Many an organizational executive or leader finds it difficult to know when he is hiring a person who is professionally competent and ethically responsible. These guidelines might prove helpful:

1. Does the Consultant Form Sound Interpersonal Relations with the Client?

A consulting relationship is based upon effective interpersonal relations. Does the consultant allow time for exploring this relationship in sufficient depth so that both parties feel that the chances are likely for developing confidence and trust? Such explorations may take place in a number of ways, but if the consultant wants long-range commitment immediately, the client may express reluctance about moving too fast into such a relationship.

2. Does the Consultant Build Dependence upon His Resources?

A responsible and ethical consultant does not make the client dependent upon him or his methods. Instead, he recognizes the need for people to solve their own problems. He will encourage these people to solve their own problems. He will encourage these people to develop their own competence and capabilities, while he gives an assist only when needed. He can do this without creating dependency.

3. Does the Consultant Try to Keep Everyone "Happy"?

Beware of the consultant who so much wants to please everyone with his work that he glosses over problems and conflict. The realities of organizational life and interpersonal dynamics mean that there will be people who feel threatened, upset and unhappy about the results of any organizational change. A consultant who wants everyone to like him or to be happy at all times may be insecure. Rather than confront management with the kinds of corrective measures it finds hard to swallow—thereby endangering his own continued employment—he dodges.

4. How Does He Talk about Other Consultants?

A sign of an unprofessional consultant is his constant derision of the talents of fellow consultants. The usual remark is: "Oh yes, I know him. He's very good in a limited fashion in the area of his narrow speciality." This blaming with faint praise is one of the key elements of the gamesmanship of the unprofessional consultant. Another good ploy might be: "Oh yes. He used to be quite competent, but he's not considered up-to-date today." A professional will not "run down" another consultant.

5. How Does the Consultant Treat the Confidences of His Past Clients?

Another sign of a charlatan is his inability to keep confidential his dealings with prior clients. This person attempts to demonstrate expertise, experience and profundity by discussing people he has run across in other organizations, or ways in which other organizations got straightened out after he was there, or the times things went from bad to worse when his advice wasn't taken. A professional does not violate the confidences of individuals or organizations in talking with other clients.

6. Is the Consultant Ambiguous About his Financial Arrangements?

One frequently finds that an unprofessional consultant will be vague about his fee or the conditions under which he will bill his services. He leaves the impression that he wants to do as much as possible for as little as possible, but then presents the client with a large bill for unspecified amounts of time and services. The true professional, on the other hand, sets ground rules for his charges so that a client knows what he is getting, what kind of services will be performed, and the rates of pay on an hourly, daily or job basis.

7. Does the Consultant Try to Seek Influence with People High Up in the Organization?

Another trait of the unprofessional consultant is his attempt to make every effort to go "over the head" of the line or staff person who brought him into the organization. This charlatan does not build the resources or respect of the department or person who brought him in but tries to relate to someone in top management. To do this, he usually goes around the person who hired him. This creates dependency (as well as building his own prestige) in the organization rather than developing the capabilities of the people he was hired to help.

8. Does the Consultant Give the Impression That He Has the Skills Necessary to Solve All Your Management Problems?

One sure sign of a non-professional is the attempt to indicate that he is not only a financial genius but an expert behavioral scientist, knowledgeable in quantitative methods and all other management sciences. He implies that you have only to tap his resources on a regular basis to have all the competence needed for running your organization in an effective way. However, many consultants who are good in one field may not be expert in the resources required to help an organization investigate the *total* aspects of its structure, finances, technology and human processes. Be wary of the consultant who unreasonably implies expansive knowledge and experience; he may be venturing far beyond the limits of his actual skills and abilities.

9. Does the Consultant Inform the Client That He is Doing One Thing When in Fact He is Doing Another?

Often an unprofessional consultant will tell the client he is getting certain results from his work when in reality he is not accomplishing that goal at all. The consultant who untruthfully indicates that he is achieving impressive results for the organization should be removed from the premises as quickly as possible.

10. Does the Consultant Express Unwillingness to Have His Services Evaluated?

One sign of the potential charlatan is an unwillingness to have his work reviewed or evaluated by persons in the organization. He will muster up comments such as: "My kind of services cannot be evaluated," or "The nature of my work is so scientific and technical that there is no way it can be accurately measured." Exercise caution with the consultant who is reluctant to get "feedback" on his own performance.

These guidelines are based on my experiences from both the sending and receiving sides of consulting services. Of course, this is not meant to be an exclusive list of unethical practices, but it is indicative of some of the concerns which should be brought to the attention of managers and organizations that hire experts in the consulting field.

In conclusion, one last guideline is worthy of comment.

11. Does the Consultant Belong to a Professional Association and/or Discipline?

A professional resource person should have a means of continually upgrading his own skills and knowledge. Membership in a discipline and/or professional association in his field is essential to assure that he is kept current in his area of expertise and that he is respected by his peers. This criterion is a key point in evaluating any resource person.

It is important to get references about a consultant from organizations other than those given as top priority by the expert himself. Any expert makes mistakes. A consultant will undoubtedly have some clients who are not pleased with his work, but in hiring this consultant it is critical to know the reasons for such displeasure. Is it a reflection of honest disagreement or is it related to one or more of the malpractices indicated above? The former is legitimate and may be an indication of a consultant who had the gumption to stand up to a client, knowing that he might risk his fee and even his reputation. The latter, on the other hand, may indicate that you have on your hands a person who is not a truly professional consultant.

Figure 2.5. Overall conference or meeting design questions to be considered.

1. Data about the participants
   a. Who is coming?
   b. What jobs or functional elements in the organiza-
      tion do they represent?
   c. How familiar they are at this moment with the
      content of the conference?
   d. What misinformation, faulty perception or wrong
      ideas do they have that need setting straight?
   e. In what areas do they need help?
   f. How can more be learned about their needs and
      expectations?
2. Data about the conference design
   a. What kind of design will best help accomplish the
      objectives?
   b. What kind of meeting facility does this design
      indicate?
   c. What are the required subparts of the meeting
      that must be accomodated?
3. Data about the conference resource persons
   a. Are "experts" needed for information giving?
   b. Are resource persons needed representative of the
      participants?
   c. Are process resource persons needed?
   d. Is a keynote speaker needed?
   e. What kinds of supporting resource people are
      needed: discussion leaders, recorders, reporters?
4. The meeting planners need to be crystal clear as to
   the following
   a. WHY the conference is being held
   b. WHAT is to be accomplished and covered, and
      what participants should be able to possess or do
      after they have attended the conference
   c. WHO in the planning group will do what
   d. HOW what is to be done will be done

Summary

Basically, the overall conference or meeting design questions that must be seen in bold perspective are given in Figure 2.5.

A meeting—any meeting—is a complicated mix of many forces. The overall perspective and design structure tries to be aware of these forces and their impact when they all come together at the meeting. It is well to reflect on the observation that was a favorite quote of Albert Einstein, "Some people will never learn anything—for this reason: they understand everything too soon."

Tim was so learned
  that he could name a horse in nine languages.
So ignorant
  that he bought a cow to ride.

Ben Franklin, Poor Richard's Almanack

3
Potpourri of Meeting Dynamics

About 15 years ago social scientists became quite interested in the forces and factors affecting meetings. The study became known as group dynamics. Quickly the focus left physical and spatial dynamics and centered on interpersonal relationships and self-knowledge and currently upon encounter experiences. In some of the earlier studies, some dynamics were identified that can usefully serve the meeting planner.

It is not the intent of this chapter to be exhaustive in the listing of such dynamics. The ones included are the ones the author, his peers and other meeting planners have often commented upon as being helpful and consciously considered by them when planning meetings. It is not often easy to identify whether the observations of these dynamics have been encountered in research studies, from personal observation, from the observation of peers or from empirical experience. If a study is not noted, it is not by design, but because at this moment in time these dynamics have become a part of meeting design considerations, the source can no longer be identified. Similarly, it should not be assumed that there is always a documented body of study to support the observations in this chapter—many of them are simply empirical.

General Dynamics

Most of the dimensions of group dynamics relate to five conditions:

1. Task conditions: Is the task fitted to the group?
2. Time conditions: Can the task be accomplished in the time available at the meeting?
3. Skill and knowledge conditions: Does the group have the skills and knowledge needed?
4. Physical facility conditions: Do the physical conditions contribute effectively to the objectives of the meeting?
5. Human relations conditions: What human behavior dynamics can dependably be predicted will operate during the meeting?

When thinking of transitions or movement of people, it is possible to move people in psychological space rather than move their bodies in physical space. Man's imagination is a wondrous thing. Through the instrument of a role play or case study or exercise, it is possible to move people to a setting a thousand miles away, to turn them within themselves or to observe a character at work who is several echelons removed from them.

Sometimes the group will need to be broken into subgroups and physically removed from each other. Despite verbal instructions to pay no attention to other individuals and groups, members in the same room can see and communicate with each other. If the group really needs privacy, it should be provided. This dynamic often relates to time and timing needs.

Related to this is still another dynamic: "How can you maintain private communications in a public place? Frequently the participant feels he cannot share and learn about his own peculiar problems. He then makes a decision about his planned behavior which may range from flight and wool-gathering to concentration on the communicator and believing that the communicator is talking to him personally. This is a mistake since it cannot happen and will result in miscommunication.

To discuss exhaustively the planning of meeting facilities is not the purpose of this discussion. However, a few comments are in order at this time:

1. More attention should be directed toward the kind of equipment needed for effective meetings.
2. How to build appropriate auditoriums, cafeterias and gymnasiums adapted also for open floor space suitable for large meeting needs should be considered.
   a. What floor surfaces can take the beating of meetings and still meet the needs of their basic purpose?
   b. How can one design functional equipment so that useful communication can occur? Most tables and chairs are heavy, difficult to store and difficult to move.
   c. Equipment should be flexible. Most equipment today is not. Trapezoidal and other shapes in tables have been experimented with; most are not a good form and are too complex. Tables shaped for easy and quick arrangement to meet the needs of the group and group communication problems are needed.
   d. Hearing and seeing is still a great problem in many rooms. The answer may lie in built-in speakers in the floor, ear plugs and on-the-table individual speakers. There is unused technology for better concentration. Similarly, means are needed to provide better projection of voices—a hand speaker every 15 feet is not the answer. Again, technology is not being utilized. The room is built and then the meeting form and purpose is fitted to meet the room's requirements—just the opposite set of conditions should obtain.
   e. Noise is disruptive. Meeting rooms are still constructed next to kitchens, busy corridors, high decibel traffic, etc. As most communicators in such situations have found, talking up does not improve the communication, it simply makes the poor communication louder.

Rooms separated by a folding door, usually plastic, are useful for some purposes, but they usually do not effectively mask normal meeting noises.

f.   It is helpful to remember that one does not solve the problem of communication with physical tools, equipment, facilities and arrangements. All that physical arrangements can do is to make it possible for a group to contribute to achieving their objectives.

There is still a tendency for meeting planners to downgrade what they variously call "administrivia" or "garbage." However, there is real validity to these parts of the meeting. For example:

1.   My serious need for a restroom break can be equated with news of the downfall of the French government or the breakdown of the organization's accounting system.
2.   Who says what is important. There is tremendous credibility in status saying something to a group. A group works differently, normally, when the president personally tells them how important their task is than when a person four echelons down reads the same message from the president.

A pattern of meeting morning and afternoon has been developed. There are interesting differences in meeting mornings with afternoons off and meeting again in the evening. Meeting times should serve the function of the meeting—not the clock.

There is a real trend toward individual learning. Mostly a learning pattern has been borrowed from the educational system— method as well as learning assumptions. The emergence of programmed instruction and confrontation training has accelerated this newer trend. Other applications suggest themselves and are often overlooked by meeting planners:

1.   Many participants do receive much learning from exhibits.

2. Organizational participants do have a need for being professionally reenergized.
3. People need time to reflect and to internalize concepts and
other program inputs.
4. One of the major benefits of a meeting is the interpersonal
communication between and among participants. This
needs to be consciously designed. There is a feeling that
every moment of the meeting must be crammed with official input. This is an absurdity and often simply defeats
the objectives of the meeting. Bull sessions, cocktail meetings, lunches and dinners—these are often the areas where
the real meeting payoff occurs.

When trying to persuade a group of 60, one does not necessarily have to feel that he is persuading 60 people. Persuasion still
basically occurs on a one-to-one basis. Group pressures make individuals conform, but often this is surface conformance. If the
resistance factor is minus 1 in each participant, many meeting
planners get trapped, when working with a group, into thinking
the resistance to overcome is minus 60. This is not true—it is
simply minus 1 for 60 participants. The techniques of one-to-one
persuasion are still valid in a group.

Most participants and leaders feel more comfortable in things
tangible and with physical arrangements such as ashtrays, dinner
and flower arrangements. But, when dealing with a dynamic system, one cannot fit adjustability and adaptability in any point of
time. For example, one can not relegate adjustability and adaptability to a point in time alone; it is needed all through the meeting
or activity.

Group Size

Once the size of the group attending the meeting is known, it
is helpful to ask, "What can I do with this size group that I cannot
do with a group of a different size?" For example, "What can I do
with 60 participants that I can not do with 15?" It is also helpful

to ask, "What are the predictable dynamics that will probably operate with a group this size?" At a very simple level, it is apparent that a group of 100 will not individually feel as responsible for the success of a meeting as will a group of 15.

For real face-to-face communications, the maximum return is reached at 15. Beyond that, no technique will do the job. Psychological distance sets in—and psychological distance cannot be measured in terms of feet and inches, but by the size of the group. Beyond 15, the phenomenon of subgroups becomes quite real, and people "feel" they are apart. Large setups only assure that people can see the program—but so do theaters. The very fact that a participant knows how many are in a group influences him, his feelings, his perceptions and his behavior.

Seating

The following kinds of observations about seating are generally valid. Participants in the back of the room know they can involve themselves in escape behavior if they want to psychologically run away from the meeting. Men will take seats nearest the doors and farther removed from the front of the room or the focus of the meeting resource persons; they generally feel lesser involved in the meeting and generally have few of the maintenance characteristics.

Two persons talking past a third person will tend to draw the third person into a conversation. So, if a less participative person is placed between two talkative persons, he will tend to participate more. Most head movements are in the direction of the right. If a talkative person is placed to the resource person's left, the resource person will tend to see him less often and therefore reduce his participation.

Elevating a person causes the listener to "look up" to him and the person talking to "look down" at the listener. Having resource persons and participants on the same floor level tends to increase identification and to lessen status differences.

Participants facing each other will talk to each other more than will participants sitting next to each other. If it is particularly

Figure 3.1. Five persons seated in semicircle with no table.

desirable to have two participants engage each other in discussion, they should be seated so that they will face each other.

A table represents a form of protection—a psychological sign that "I have something I can lean on—fend you off—hide under—." A table can be, to the group and the discussion or task, either a barrier or a support. The author looked at this phenomenon during a laboratory group experience at Bethel, Maine.*

Seated at a round table, it is more difficult to locate a leadership position. A table is, in a sense, a kind of semicommunication line. The contour of the table establishes communications. People have no label for this. It can, of course, be a threat as well as a promise. For example, five people are placed in a semicircle, sitting in chairs but with no table, as in Figure 3.1. Under these conditions with the assumption that there is no formally designated or organizational leader, it is generally impossible to determine who will assume the leadership role.

But if the same seating positions are maintained and a rectangular table is inserted, as in Figure 3.2, one can predict who will probably be selected leader or will assume the leadership role. Leadership is associated with the end of a table. Similarly, other predictions can be made.

---

*Leslie E. This, "The Sub-Table Meeting," *Adult Leadership* 9, no. 9 (March 1961):269-95.

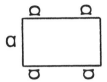

Figure 3.2. Five persons seated in semicircle at table.

1. Participants will associate the end of a room containing the blackboard, easel or stage with the "business end" of the room. Those who want to get involved sit toward this end; those who do not want involvement sit at the opposite end.
2. A woman normally will be appointed a recorder or secretary.
3. In a male group, the male with paper and pencil in evidence will normally be appointed the recorder.

A skirt around a table usually makes the participants feel more comfortable, especially women and girls.

Time

The larger the group, the more the task must be tailored and fitted to the size. This has implications not only for the availability of real time but also for the capability of the group to use time. What is the advantage of a three-hour meeting where people are 15 minutes late and horse around for 30 minutes more versus a fast-moving two-hour meeting?

After approximately 1½ hours of meeting, the productivity of a group tapers off. Another half hour and it falls off sharply. A rule of thumb is that a movement by a participant more often than one per minute indicates boredom or fatigue. Few people can concentrate longer than two to three minutes at a stretch; then they need a let-up. Observe comedians at work and their pacing of material, and you will observe an excellent example of the operation of this phenomenon.

Physical Facility

A physical facility sets a mental mood for a meeting—either positive or negative. A number of training directors have commented that when they locate a training session at a college or university, the participants study, read and participate with more concentration than when the training session is located at a motel, hotel or resort.

Physical facilities can be too plush and comfortable. Participants can concentrate better, participate more effectively and remain more mentally alert when there is a trace of discomfort. Chairs can be too comfortable. The chairs, table and room can be distracting or too alluring. Meeting in a somber board room replete with formal, massive-legged mahogany table and pictures of austere organizational patriarchs staring from the walls can stifle informality and creativity.

One of the few articles dealing with the dynamic of the physical facility was written in 1968 by Fred I. Steele, "The Impact of the Physical Setting on the Social Climate at Two Comparable Laboratory Sessions."* This article is reprinted because of its significant observations and implications of these observations.

Introduction

There is a steadily growing interest among behavioral scientists in exploring and understanding the complex relationship between man and his physical world—the way in which the environment influences individ-

_____

*Fred I. Steele, "The Impact of the Physical Setting on the Social Climate at Two Comparable Laboratory Sessions," *Human Relations Training News* 12, no. 4 (1968). Reprinted by permission of the publisher.

ual behavior, interaction, and so on, and the ways in which human behavior changes the environment for better or worse.

I think that in the laboratory training process we generate a tremendous amount of unused information about the impact of the environment on behavior. The climate of inquiry, expanded awareness, and experimentation that is fostered at a laboratory session would seem to be ideal for the collection of data about persons' experiences with the physical spaces that define their world for the duration of the laboratory. They tend to be more willing and able to articulate what they are experiencing and to try out new spatial relationships to see what differences they make. Also, since the laboratory sessions are often held in relatively self-contained locations (the "cultural island"), the impact of the physical setting is in clearer focus than it would be if we were trying to understand how New York City affects participants (a slightly more complex problem).

In this brief report I should like to describe a fortuitous "natural" field experiment with two laboratory settings and to indicate some of the environmental influences that seemed to be important. The two sessions were identical in terms of purpose: to train members of a large metropolitan service organization to be better action change agents in their community work settings. Two sessions were held, rather than one, simply to keep the size down; there were from 45 to 50 persons in each session. The laboratory design for each also was the same: to focus on the task of building a learning community and to learn from the emergent dynamics of that situation. The participant population were roughly matched, since they were chosen randomly for the two sessions from a pool of persons who were to take part in the program. Each session's participants were about 75 per cent male, 65 per cent white, and 35 per cent black.

There was a big difference, however, in the physical settings of the two sessions. Since they were fairly compatible on the dimensions of goals, design, and population characteristics, it therefore seemed likely that we could learn about environmental impact by comparing the mood and outcomes of the two sessions. The remainder of this article will describe the two settings (called A and B for convenience), articulate some of the main climate differences which the staff observed, and suggest some of the principal environmental factors that helped to account for these differenes in climate.

Setting A. This was a large, multipurpose camp setting. It was on the shores of a lake, with fairly hilly and varied terrain in the vicinity of the camp. There were trees and open spaces, with paths and walkways winding among the various buildings and converging on the central dining–meeting building from the living areas. One living building was low, like a motel, the other was two-storied, with four adjacent rooms on each story. The rooms in each building could accommodate as many as four persons. In the dining room there were large tables with a seating capacity of 20, and the main meeting room was in the same building, opposite the entrance to the dining room.

Setting B. This session was held in a new, highrise nine-story building in a light industrial area outside the metropolitan downtown area. The living quarters essentially were single rooms on Floors 2-8. There were a cafeteria, pool, and gymnasium on the ground floor. The cafeteria tables were varied and smaller, seating from two to six. The main meeting room was on the top floor, and generally was reached by an elevator. The surroundings of the building had a few places to walk down residential street, and a major highway ran in front of the building.

Climate Differences in the Two Sessions

Basically, a sense of community and shared responsibility developed in A but not in B. Meetings or events of various kinds were held regularly in A; there was a sense of continually working on the task and struggling with issues such as the black-white intergroup problems. In B, meetings were sporadic, slow to start, and often attended by fewer than half of the community. In A there was a concern for housing, the implications of various living arrangements, and experimentation with new patterns as the session went on. In B, there was only a "mechanical" concern that everyone have a bed (even if he did not want it) and no experimentation once everyone had his own room. There were expressed community concerns in A for those who were on the periphery or had dropped out—this was seen as something for which the community should take responsibility and which the members could help to improve. In B there was no expressed concern for those who were out, and indeed because of the lack of cohesion it was difficult to tell how many "casualties" there were.

There was a sense of joy, spontaniety, and fun in A, but little of this (at least little observable) in B, with practically no transmission of fun from one group to another. In B, cliques formed early and remained fixed, with little variation; in A, there was a more fluid shuffling of relationships and contacts, with cliques coming together to form larger subgroups, then reforming into new patterns.

The Impact of the Environment

Since the two populations basically were the same, it seems a good assumption that at least some of the differences between the two climates resulted from the differences in the physical settings. One dimension which seemed important was observability or visibility: In A, it was high—people could see others coming and going because of the path arrangements and open spaces at ground level. In B, the single rooms and corridors on different floors made observation of others' movements very difficult—most of the flow was in the encapsulated steel boxes called elevators, and an individual could not get a feel for where the community was moving at any given time.

Another dimension was the juxtaposition of the main common facilities. In A, the closeness of the dining room and the main meeting room made it likely that people would naturally gather together soon after a meal. As for B, there was not such closeness and little likelihood that people would naturally go to the meeting room, drawn by the presence of others whom they could see there (observability again). More initiative was required (going up eight floors) to find out whether anything was happening.

The living arrangements themselves provided another factor: Persons in B were placed in single rooms and thus had less contact with one another; if they were feeling low or frustrated, they tended to withdraw to their rooms, thereby not receiving new inputs from others that might have helped them move off dead center. In A, the group living pattern provided opportunities for a person to receive inputs from others, both those in his room and those in the nearby cluster of rooms.

Average contact or interaction also was lower in B because there were few natural gathering places other than the main meeting room, which was associated with work and frustration. Little gathering could take place in the narrow halls or small rooms, and the cafeteria allowed space for only small groupings that were necessarily time-bounded because customers not involved in the laboratory were being served.

A final difference that seemed to be important was simply the higher aesthetic quality of the A setting. It had natural beauty and was conducive to participants' relaxing and moving about with one another. The nonnatural setting and lack of easy movement in B seemed to produce a cooped-up feeling that was not relieved by an enjoyment of the environment itself, which had a view of the whole metropolitan skyline. And the fact that this was the main "work" place probably made for a poor combination since people felt under pressure while there and may have used the view as a way of escaping from the task ambiguity that they were reluctant to face. This last effect also suggests an important clarifying point—that the physical setting will have a different effect in one social environment from that in another—that it is the interaction between the physical and social factors that creates the psychological environment for an individual at a given time. The emphasis here has been on the influence of the physical space, on the social climate, but it is clear that there are many forces pushing in the opposite direction as well. (We can all recall personal experiences where no amount of quality in our physical surroundings could overcome the basically negative influence of the social climate.) Hopefully, one outcome of the discussion here will be to encourage more of us to get the physical and social factors working in the same (desired) direction.

Finally, this hope suggests that there were really two reasons for my interest in the events that are described here. I began by calling for the use of the training laboratory's potential to generate new knowledge about the impact of the physical environment on human attitudes and behavior. The second potential that I think is illustrated here is the potency of physical design to influence the quality of learning experiences at a laboratory session. I think we could do much better at creating facilitative learning environments if we were to work at using the setting as an integral part of the mix of influences working for change, rather than just doing a superficial once-over when we choose a place and cursory evaluation of the setting when the session is finished.

Not only is there an art in knowing a thing,
but also a certain art in teaching it.

Cicero, Do Legibus

4
Conference
Methods

After who is coming to the meeting and their expectations are
known and meeting objectives have been tightly defined, the next
concern is with the questions, "What method(s) will best help
achieve these objectives?" It should be noted that a book concerned with planning meetings should deal with the planning process in some kind of sequential order. Further, to focus thinking, it
is desirable to discuss these steps separately. However, the planning process does not proceed so cleanly or neatly.

The mechanistic steps in planning or decision making are often
discussed separately: define the problem, collect data, develop
alternatives, etc. Any planner or decision maker knows it does not
happen this way. One collects data while still defining the problem; implementation matters concern him while developing alternatives. The same is true in meeting planning. One does not finish
the step of determining who is coming, then consider objectives,

then consider methodology and so on. These matters have a way of being interrelated. The mosaic of the completed meeting is constantly shifting before the planner's eyes. But, he will find that his major concerns will tend to be sequential.

A simple truism is this: methods should always work to help the planner accomplish the meeting objectives. There is too often a tendency to "latch on" to a method because it is popular this year, with little concern or questioning whether it is in any way related to the meeting content or objectives. It is at this point form is permitted to carry content—or to mask the lack of content. If one really has something worthwhile to say, participants will let him say it under adverse conditions and not be too critical. If someone is lost on a rainy night, he will gratefully accept directions from a shabby man who speaks broken English and has a most unpleasant platform appearance.

One problem that must be confronted is the simple question, "What is a method?" Numerous techniques exist to assist the meeting planner, but which should be called "methods"; which should be called "meeting aids"; and which should be called "meeting techniques." No generally accepted definition or listing of methods is known. For example, is the "Phillips 66" a method or simply a technique? Some try to make sense out of the problem by listing "methods" according to whether they "tell," "show" or involve "doing." Others just list them willy-nilly. Still others differentiate "type of meeting" from "method" from "technique." Often the differences in terminology are extremely minor.

Dr. Leonard Nadler* also acknowledges this difficulty when he comments:

---

*Leonard Nadler, *Developing Human Resources* (Houston: Gulf Publishing Company, 1970), pp. 182-83.

Once again, there is a lack of agreement on terminology. The varying backgrounds of individuals engaged in HRD (human resource development), the confusion as to its boundaries and the lack of a recognized body of knowledge all contribute to this confusion. Attempts have been made among various kinds of adult educations to bring some order out of this confusion. Coolie Verner has contributed by recommending:

Method: the organization of the learning experience (i.e., class meeting)

Technique: the process for facilitating learning (i.e., role play, group discussion, panel, etc.)

Device: the mechanical instruments to augment the methods and techniques (i.e., audio-visuals, physical arrangements)

The general use of these terms would be helpful. However, it is not certain that there is enough agreement among the readers to use them in this discrete fashion. Rather than become embroiled at this point and miss the essence of what the instructor does, the term "methodology" will be used to encompass all three.

A matrix has been designed that seems to make sense but is not without its problems. For the purpose of this discussion, a matrix will be used that differentiates:

1. Kinds of meetings
2. Methods involving one person
3. Methods involving dyads and triads
4. Methods involving small groups (five to 15)
5. Methods involving any size group
6. Techniques that do not seem to warrant being called methods

In choosing a method or technique, it helps to remember that 100 people in a group can be either used to work on a problem in 100 ways, or 100 people can work on a problem together. The method employed relates to purpose and objective.

The meeting planner needs

1. To have a wide familiarity with methods and techniques,
2. To use primarily those that contribute to meeting objectives,
3. If possible, to vary methods to heighten interest and avoid participant boredom

Methods are critical tools for the meeting planner. Some are designed to impart information, to change attitudes and behavior, to improve or to learn new skills, to solve a problem or to get action, while others are intended to integrate all these change targets. It would be useful to list the various meeting methods and techniques under these five headings and refer to it after the meeting objectives were determined.

One other consideration is cardinal. Most meeting participants are becoming quite sophisticated about meeting methods and techniques. They attend many meetings; their children talk about methods and techniques used at school and in their groups; and they read about them. Many are surfeited with exposure to techniques involving bells, chimes, prizes, animated movement and activity, dancing girls and expensively packaged visuals. There is increasing disenchantment with entertainment and a desire for meaningful content.

However, it still remains true that participants vary widely in the methods with which they feel comfortable and which enable them to get the most out of meetings. Although no research is known to support this observation, it is believed, from experience in meetings, training and education, that participants fall roughly into two groups:

1. Those who are "thing" and "result" centered. People, processes, diagnosis, reflection and discovering their own learning leave them cold. They are bored by personal introductions—"Just give your name and company." They love to take notes and receive handouts. Their preferred method is the lecture or presentation. After small group discussions they are the ones who say, "You could have told us that in three minutes. Why did you have us spend an hour in small groups?" Meeting planners who are so oriented will ask a resource person "to deal with the entire concept of motivation. We are listing you on the program from 9:03 to 9:11."

2. Those who are "people," "process" and "self-discovery" learning oriented. These participants do not like presentations or lectures. Usually they are non-note takers. They will accept presentations and handouts as useful for "cognitive maps." They like small groups, discussion, exercises, role plays and all kinds of interpersonal interactions. They love to discover things for themselves—no matter that the thing discovered appears all through the literature. Feelings are important to them. They love conceptual work and the discovery of new relationships.

No known way exists to please both of these broad preferences and method expectations. If a meeting is designed fully in one direction, half the group will be lost. If it is designed in the other direction, the other half will be lost. Often balancing the methodology has been tried—with the usual result that neither group is completely happy. It is increasingly felt that the answer lies, where this is possible, in the screening and selection of participants. Often this is not possible since all persons in the organization subunit or functional group must attend the meeting. Under these conditions, the meeting planner must know the participants' preferences in how they learn best from meetings and skew his methodology in this direction. With time, it is possible slowly to reorient the "thing" oriented participants toward the "people" methodologies. Another useful device is to employ the two-track meeting system—have concurrent kinds of sessions to cover the same content.

In selecting methodologies, the meeting planner should constantly keep in mind that he is training or educating adults—not children. The orientation of adults toward a meeting or learning is quite different than that of a child (though there is a fair amount of evidence that this is changing). Among these differences, the following are most often mentioned:

1. There is little difference in the physiological resources between a child and adult except slower reaction time by the adult. This has always appeared to us to be too simply stated. Leonard Nadler* deals with this dimension in a more realistic view—by acknowledging what others often overlook—that there are realities like age and defective hearing and sight.
2. Adults must want to learn and will engage in a learning situation only when this is true. Children will often engage in learning when they do not want to.
3. Adults seem to learn best by doing. "Doing may be a shortcut to learning, and the adult is more interested in the results than an understanding of the theory and dynamics. This often results in the adult looking for the universal "answer" or "gimmick."
4. Adults like to work on real life problems but in so doing constantly run the risk of becoming "content seduced."
5. Adults, obviously, have more experience than children and, with the proper use of methodology, can draw upon this experience to enrich a meeting. It is not unusual, with a group of 25 in an organizational meeting, to find 500 years of experience represented in the group. Of course, one must beware of the phenomenon of one year's experience repeated 20 times.

* Ibid.

6. Adults generally learn best in a non-school environment. However, the data is really not clear. Some participants learn best by lecture and the classroom environment of discipline and authority; others learn best in an informal setting discovering their own learnings.

7. Adults seem more interested in guidance and results than in grades. It has been observed that adults like to know how they are doing and how they rate with others or a norm but do not want their grades or scoring shared with other participants. Often they do not even want to share this information with the resource leader.

Major Kinds of Meetings

Generally, each meeting will have an overall purpose which broadly indicates the kinds of methodologies and techniques which should be employed. The term applied to the meeting, then, creates expectations of what the meeting is about and the kinds of activities in which the participant can expect to be engaged. The following are more common kinds of meetings.

Clinic. A meeting in which a very specific content or phenomenon will be studied is the clinic. Primarily the participants expect to be in a "learner" role with the meeting being conducted by professionals in the content area. Experiences of the participants will be utilized but are anticipated to be minor. It is highly diagnostic—for example, a clinic to consider "The Effect of ADP upon Hourly Employees."

Conference. As the term conference implies, the sponsoring group wants to confer with the participants. The purpose of the conferring can be multiple: confer about a problem, confer about procedures, confer about how a decision or plan is working, confer on how to sell more products, etc. Specialists will give information, but much information and input are expected from participants. Sometimes the meeting planners are heavy on input and use the participants to test proposed organizational matters. The conference may also be used to solve a problem, to make a decision or to provide an opportunity for participants to share experiences.

Sometimes it is used simply to bring participants up to date on what has happened within the organization since the last time they met. Often more than one of these objectives are involved.

Convention. Usually a convention is a formal annual meeting of the group. Part of the content is the conduct of organizational business—the "business meeting." It is usually formal in nature, involves large numbers of participants and is run by protocol and specific rules of order. Other objectives—often educational activities and information giving—may be included; but the major purpose is the conduct of organizational affairs.

Institute. An institute is designed primarily for learning purposes. Participants expect to be in a learning posture and to have resource persons with expertise in their fields. It is seen as an educational experience normally outside the framework of an accredited system. It may, of course, be held on an educational institution campus, but normally no academic credit for completing the program is expected.

Laboratory. A laboratory is a meeting in which participants expect primarily to learn from others, self and trainer. The trainer's role is to facilitate learning and to set conditions under which self-learning can occur. Generally, it involves the content of social scientists, not physical scientists. The basic content is the "here and now" rather than the "there and then."

Seminar. In a seminar a group of experienced people meet with one or more knowledgeable resource persons to discuss a given content area. The participants are expected to be quite knowledgeable, and resource persons expect to learn from them. A great deal of information and experience is exchanged. Often there is more expertise in the participants than in the resource persons. It is not expected that either problem solving, action or planning will necessarily result from the meeting.

Symposium. Several points of views or kinds of experiences are systematically presented in the symposium. Usually the major thrust is "airing" a number of views and collecting data (it is not normally expected that any simple view or action program will emerge). It does allow for a limited subject area to be explored in depth. A symposium is relatively unstructured and does not provide for the subject matter to be neatly diagramed or conceptualized.

Work Conference. Participants in the work conference—sometimes simply called "a meeting"—are from the same organization, and usually the resource persons are middle and top management or heads of functional and staff areas. The purpose is to confront organizational problems and to become familiar with operating manuals, procedures, policies, implementation, etc. Often the work conference involves detailed examination of processes and systems. The end objective is to achieve better organizational knowledge and functioning. Education in the broad sense is not an objective.

Workshop. The main purpose of the workshop is to learn how to do something better or to understand something better. Participants adopt the role of learners. Resource persons have high expertise and behave as instructors. The workshop may include the learning of skills and thus involve much practice; example: "Workshop in Jewelry Making"; "Workshop in Secretarial Skills"; "Workshop in PERT."

Groupings

One learning method is that of discussion groups. However, the gamut of group sizes, group composition and group purposes are almost endless. For that reason, it seems desirable to look at the more common subgroupings employed.

The name given to the group depends upon the primary purpose to which the group and/or its discussion is to be directed. If they are to observe something, they will be called "observation groups." Often the composition will vary according to the purpose, as will the group size. The mechanics employed will also vary with the group and its purposes—for example, whether the group uses a chairman, reporter, recorder, discussion leader, secretary, etc. It has been found more useful to think of the following groups as each utilizing not separate methodologies or techniques but refinements of a basic method—that of small groups. They could, of course, be broken down into two major categories:

1. Groups basically meant to discuss something with a specific focus;
2. Groups formed for basic purposes other than to discuss something.

They are not so broken down. These two broad categories lend themselves to other subcategories and, if this tack is followed, defeats the purpose of looking at groupings of participants as one conference method. The following are the groupings most frequently encountered.

Application Groups. As the name implies, the application group applies new information, new skills, new attitudes or whatever has been taught.

Buzz Groups. Often the term, buzz group, is used as a synonym for "discussion group." More specifically it has come to mean a quick, informal discussion, usually with one or two others and during a formal presentation. It is used quite broadly in both these contexts. It is generally used for a task that can be accomplished quickly, to get immediate data, to test application of a concept or point made in the presentation, as a "warm-up" or for involvement.

Diagnostic group. The diagnostic group is used to diagnose a problem, situation, process, event or itself. It searches for causes and effects. Increasingly, it is used in connection with laboratory training.

Listening Team. Three to nine people who listen to the resource person or presenter through a specifically assigned filter comprises the listening team. For example, in a group of three, one person can be asked to listen for what is not being said, another for what he disagrees with, another for how he thinks the customer would react to the content. This is then fed back to the total group or resource person for response. Sometimes the entire audience is divided into teams—"You folks in this section listen to the presentation from the point of view: What does the presenter not say I think he should have said"; "You folks in this section from the point of view: What does the presenter say I heartily disagree with"; etc.

Occupational Groups. The small occupational group is composed on the basis of the participants' occupations. "All typists will form Group A, all machinists will form Group B and all lawyers will form Group C." This is done to analyze content or concepts through occupational eyes, to assure that semantic problems will be reduced or to provide similarity of examples and application.

Off-the-Record Group. More on the nature of a bull session, the off-the-record group can be more candid since they know they will not report to the total group.

Orientation Group. To help new members get acquainted, to introduce participants to content with which they are unfamiliar, to explain how the meeting will work, or to introduce and to familiarize with anything that is new to the participants—these are the purposes of the orientation group.

Phillips 66. Primarily a device to divide a large audience into discussion groups easily, Phillips 66 has three in a row turn to three in the row behind—this gives a group of six. If done uniformly, audience should quickly be divided into discussion groups of six.

Problem- Solving Group. In addition to discussion, problem-solving group is asked to solve a specific problem. The solution of a problem takes priority over all other functions of the small group.

Reactor Panel. A small group appointed by resource person or by total group, the purpose of the reactor panel is to "react" to the presentation and to represent the audience. At the conclusion of his presentation, the resource person turns to the panel who reacts. The resource person responds. Sometimes the audience may send points up to the reactor panel for them to raise.

Reality-Testing Group. Members of the reality-testing group either respond to the presenter on the reality of his input or role-play a concept after the presentation to test its applicability.

Round-Table Group. Simply a small discussion group seated around a round table, the round-table group now more often seems to mean simply a discussion group.

Skill-Practice Group. Members of the skill-practice group have the opportunity to practice a new skill or behavior. It may be an individual or a group skill. They have a chance to see how it feels and to obtain feedback on their effectiveness. This group may or may not be conducted with the aid of an experienced "supervisor."

Platform Group. Members of this small group on platform discuss among themselves the presentation after they have heard it. The assumption is that their discussion will reflect the responses of the audience and will also stimulate the audience's applications of the concepts in the presentation.

Special Interest Group. Sometimes used to include those who have a special interest in the subject, sometimes on the basis of functional interest, sometimes on the basis of common interest, the special interest group looks at the assignment through the special eyes of this interest. Often these groups do not report back to the total group.

Study Group. Usually simply another name for discussion group, the study group sometimes "studies" an article or book—usually preassigned reading. Very often the group either reports back to the total group or leads the total group in a discussion of the material it studied.

Work Group. The term, work group, may also be simply another name for discussion group. Sometimes the assignment or expectation is that the members will determine facts, study application and make recommendations. Usually they are expected to report to the total group. Sometimes the group is given a live organization problem to work out.

Methods Involving a Single Participant

Because group methods have been the main focus in recent years, an elementary fact has almost been forgotten: an individual can learn by himself without interacting with other people. Indeed, there seems to be increasing evidence that some people learn many things better alone than in a group. The following are among the methodologies utilized for individual learning.

Reading. This may be assigned as preliminary reading or reading during a session.

Programmed Instruction. Textual or machine, programmed instruction may be done in advance or during the meeting.

Completion of Instruments. Performed in advance or during the meeting, completion of instruments includes check lists, true/ false statements, profiles preparation, etc.

Reflection. Seldom is reflection listed as a method, but it can be useful not so much to learn something new as to integrate and internalize learnings.

Interviewer. Interviewing a single participant is not really a method. (It is included here because it does not fit the other categories.) Sometimes a participant is asked to interview other participants or resource persons or those with expertise. The data collected may primarily be his property or can be shared with the total group.

Guided Experience. Normally done with one participant, the guided experience seldom involves more than five. The participant receives individually supervised assistance in learning a job function, skill or interpersonal behavior skill.

In-Basket Exercise. An example of an exercise, the in-basket exercise involves a number of prepared items that require action or a decision. Participants initially work alone against a time limit. Usually about 20 items, some interrelated, are in the "in-basket." The number will not permit detailed handling of all items. Sometimes one of the items changes the parameters of the job—as when one item announces the participant's secretary has become suddenly ill and has left the office. The exercise usually tests knowledge of the organization's policies and regulations, decision making, response to working under pressure, etc.

Other methods also involve the individual participant and often cause him to work alone. Examples would be gaming and case studies. They are not included here since they are almost always used as part of preparation for later involvement with a larger group. The methods discussed in this section assume that the participant will not necessarily interact with other participants as a result of his work or study.

Methods Involving Dyads and Triads

Two of the most effective groupings are dyads and triads. It is surprising what participants will share with one or two other participants that they will not share with three or more persons. The dynamics in dyads and triads are significantly different from those of larger groups. The following are among the methodologies frequently employed for these groupings.

Consulting Teams. Two or three participants are appointed to form a consulting team. They may work on home or other real problems and use the other member(s) to provide consultation. Another common usage is to practice the skill of interviewing: one member takes the role of the client, another the role of interviewer and the third the role of observer. After 10 minutes of interview, the observer feeds back his observations. Roles are changed so that all three play all three roles. Many variations of this method exist.

Neighbor Discussions. Groups of two or three compare notes during breaks provided by discussion leader, resource person or presenter. They stimulate the thinking of each other.

Observation Team. Two or three participants, as an observation team, observe a common phenomenon—for example, a staff meeting. Often the focus desired is instrumented. They then meet to compare notes, test the validity of each other's findings and stimulate the thinking of each other and suggest ways of improving needed skills or behavior. Sometimes they report their findings back to the total group.

Methods Applicable to Groups of Varying Sizes

Several methods exist for group learning. The following are some examples of these various methodologies.

Case Study. A case, or incident, is presented verbally, in narrative form, by film, by video tape, by records or by a skit in the case study method. Usually individuals study the case, analyze it and recommend actions. These are then discussed in small groups;

a group decision is arrived at; and in a total group the case and recommendations are presented and analyzed with the help of a case leader. The case can be simple or complex and can be studied and restudied. The method requires ample time for analysis and comprehension of the situation. It often is assigned the evening before the session, and participants work on the case as an evening assignment.

Colloquy. Directed discussion of an issue or problem by a capable leader with the audience constitutes a colloquy. Frequently, the pertinent questions to be asked are preselected. Occasionally the discussion leader is called an "interlocutor." He may use a listening team or reactor panel to assist him. If questions of procedure arise, or there is a need to determine the "right" answer, the discussion leader makes these decisions. Sometimes the term simply is used in a broad sense to mean collective inquiry by a group with a leader. The method seems to have declined in usage the past 10 years.

Confrontation. A fairly new method, confrontation assumes that the primary responsibility for learning is on the individual. When the participant arrives at the meeting, he goes through several "confrontations" to see how he handles them. For example, in a booth he may find a customer, on film, posing a question to him. He replies to the question, and his answer is tape-recorded. Either he scores himself as to how well he did, or the tape is scored by others with expertise. If he passes, he goes on to other confrontations. If he does not pass, he schedules an appointment to repeat the confrontation. He prepares for the confrontation by reading, by talking to experts, by film, by studying organizational manuals, etc. The participant, then, selects his own training needs to work on and stops when he is satisfied he has learned enough. Many variations of the method exist.

Court Technique. The method, that of a court case and scene, utilizes a judge, witness and chief attorneys—one for the issue and one against. A question, issue, concept, decision, plan or something similar is the matter to be "tried." It follows the court procedure, including calling witnesses for both sides. The judge rules on matters of procedure. Both chief attorneys "sum up" their arguments after 25 to 40 minutes of the trial. After the trial, the audience may query the attorneys and may be requested to render a "verdict." This method seemed more popular some years ago than today.

Demonstration. An expert shows how something should be done or how something works in a demonstration. Often used with hardware and equipment, it may also be used with human behavior or techniques. The demonstration is often followed up with supervised practice sessions.

Drill and Practice. Usually the term drill and practice is applied to practice involving manual skills, such as typing, welding, etc. It can also refer to human relationship skills, such as telephone manners, interviewing and public speaking.

Debate. In a debate, an issue is discussed before an audience, either by two individuals or two teams. They alternate in presenting their positions and arguments. Usually a moderator rules on points of order. The form is highly stylized and is slanted toward "winning" rather than communicating. Its most useful feature is that it forces out all sides of an issue. Its major drawback is that "winning" often hinges on "cuteness," semantics, verbal and logic tricks.

Encounter Training. This methodology, encounter training, means many different things to many different people. The flavor of encounter training can be seen in an announcement for a one-week program, "Encounter for Singles," announced in a recent catalog.

Participants will explore their self-concepts and define the imagined limits they set for being most fully and vibrantly themselves. In a supportive context of openness and honesty, group members will give each other feedback, encourage acceptance of what is, and the taking of appropriate risks to be who and what they want. We will explore "shoulds" and "oughts" to find realistic personal definitions of commitment and responsibility. . . .As need arises, such methods as psychodrama, meditation, sense awareness exercises, body movement, fantasy and Gestalt technique will be used. . . .Methods will be used for participants to discover themselves in open and honest relationships.

Exercise. An exercise is usually a complex role play or combination role play/case study which may last for a half day or a full day. For example, an entire community may be replicated, objectives are set for various groups and interactions occur as they would in real life. There may be manipulation of roles of individuals or groups; time limits are set for various phases of the exercise; judges and umpires rule on mechanics. Participants get a "feel" of the real life situation and later analyze the dynamics they identified and their behavior and speculate on ways a change in strategy, tactics or behavior could have altered the outcome. Often the term describes simple "pieces of experience"—from filling out an organizational form to solving a puzzle.

Field Trip. Participants go to an actual site, location or plant on a field trip to observe firsthand a live operation. For example, participants may be taken to a distillery to see how whisky is made.

Forum. In a forum, an issue is presented to the audience by one or more knowledgeable resource persons. Usually the resource persons make formal presentations prepared in advance. Frequently the resource persons present conflicting positions. The meeting is then opened to the audience who question the resource persons as well as each other. It is more formal than a panel.

Forum Dialogue. Two, sometimes more, people carry on a discussion about a topic or issue in a forum dialogue. They may or may not be in basic agreement. When most of their contributions have been presented, the audience is invited to participate in the discussion.

Gaming. The context of gaming is that of "war games." Real life is replicated, and a series of decisions are to be made by the participants either individually or in groups. Specific times are alloted for making the decision, and then a decision must be made.

Participants may be given several variables before each decision point to see how well they can handle them as well as to see if they are high or low risk takers. Normally one or more judges or umpires are utilized to handle the game and to rule on matters of procedure, interpretation and related matters. Games may be either manual or computerized. Since they tend to be scored easier if they deal with quantifiable matters or items predictable or "hard," they tend to be used in business and industry more than in the social sciences or human behavior areas. Participants may play to win among themselves, or they may "play" the system or the computer.

Group Discussion. Called by many names, including "huddle groups," "round-table groups," "buzz groups," etc., discussion groups are usually groups of five to seven members who discuss an issue, concept or meeting input. The purposes may vary widely as was seen when "groupings" were discussed. There may be a designated group leader, or the group may appoint its own. Usually the main points or findings of the group are reported by a recorder or the chairman to the total group. The skills and knowledge necessary to accomplish the group's task must reside in the individuals —a point often overlooked by meeting planners. Too often, insufficient time is provided for the group to work, resulting in shallow findings.

Incident Process. Participants receive an incident and are to solve the problem posed in the incident process—a variation of the case study. They may ask the leader for data which only he possesses. If they ask for the right data, they should be able to solve the problem. The "textbook" answer is supplied at the end of the case. The method tests the ability of participants to engage in effective and pertinent fact-finding. Individuals may arrive at a decision and check this out with others in a small group or with the total group.

In-Basket Exercise. See "Methods Involving a Single Participant." The method lends itself best to complex cases. The initial incident may be presented by narrative, role play, movie, video tape, record, etc.

Laboratory. A learning method that utilizes the behavior of the persons in the learning activity to analyze their "here and now" experiences as the prime focus of the content of their learning—this is the laboratory method.

Lecture. A prepared presentation by a speaker, the lecture may or may not be supported by visuals. It may or may not be followed by a question period. Sometimes the speaker will discuss a main point and then invite questions, or he may allow questions at any time. Another way of handling questions is to "plant" them in the audience—questions the presenter wants to be sure are asked. Often the audience writes out questions which are collected and screened by the moderator. This weeds out crank and duplicate questions. The method is particularly useful to impart new knowledge in an organized fashion. The speaker may also serve what Donald K. Smith, when he was president of the Central State Speech Association (Minnesota), called a "symbolic healer"; that is, organizational groups need secular evangelism to "reduce the tension, frustrations, and possible feelings of guilt arising inevitably from the structure of a highly organized, highly specialized and competitive business community."

Marathon Training. Training that continues for an extended period of time with no scheduled breaks, marathon training may continue from 12 hours to seven days. Participants eat, sleep and study in the meeting room(s). It seems particularly adapted to objectives to change behavior and attitudes.

Film/Audio-Visual Tape Involvement. Until recent years film was primarily used to present "the great face" or simulate real life incidents. There is an increasing trend to design film so the audience is involved. This may mean posing questions for later discussion, building the film as an integral part of a three-hour session, stopping the film and having participants react or fill out instruments to be used later, etc. A recent example is the Bureau of National Affairs' series, "Organization Renewal," featuring Dr. Gordon L. Lippitt. Occasionally commercial films are used that have high emotional impact and are designed into behavioral training. One much used example is the film, "Twelve Angry Men."

Panel. Three to five "experts" discuss an issue or topic in the panel method. Normally opposing views are represented. Participants may open with three to 10-minute prepared statements and then engage each other in a discussion. After 30 to 45 minutes the audience is invited to ask questions of the panel. A moderator is used to keep time, to rule on questions of procedure and to introduce the panel members. It is useful to have some rehearsal, but care must be taken not to rehearse so much as to drain the exchanges of vitality and informality. However, panel members should know the major points and positions of the other panel members. Sometimes the prepared three to 10-minute statements of panel members are shared in advance with the other members.

Play. Professional actors, or good amateurs, may act out a well-written play to illustrate a problem, dilemma, situation, etc. The audience uses the play data for their discussions. The major advantage is that it realistically portrays feelings and the milieu of the "real life" situation.

Practice Session. See "Drill and Practice."

Problem Solving. The premise in problem solving is that participants learn by working on real problems. As they work on organizational problems, periodically they examine the dynamics and processes involved. Many names are given to this basic method: the American National Red Cross called it "situational training"; Robert Blake's Grid System would fall into this category; and the current process being called organization development or organizational renewal would also be examples.

Project. Sometimes the individual participant, or a small group, is given a specific project or assignment on which to work. The assumption is made that learning will occur as they work on the project. Term papers, book reviews or any specially assigned task would fall into this category. The project may be accomplished under the supervision of a capable resource person, or the participant(s) may work on his own and have his results evaluated by a resource person.

Role Play. Participants "act out" an incident or a situation. The roles and situation may be written out in detail. More frequently the situation and role is sketched briefly, and the role player "fills in" the role. It can be used to have others see how a situation or piece of behavior looks and used for later discussion and analysis. More often it is used to help the role player get a firsthand "feel" of what it is like to be in a given situation or to behave in a given way. Sometimes the role players reverse roles. Another favorite device is to use alter egos to indicate what the role players are really feeling and thinking at a given moment. The method is an outgrowth of psychodrama—used extensively in mental hospitals and for therapy purposes in WWII.

Sensitivity Training. An application of the laboratory method, sensitivity training uses an unstructured group learning experience to facilitate the participant in learning the effect of his behavior on others, the effect of other persons' behavior on his, and self-understanding.

Symposium. In the symposium several resource persons, usually not more than four or five, make brief presentations on various aspects of a subject, topic, concept or other item. A moderator normally summarizes. Respondents may also be used to critique each, or all, the papers or presentations. Questions from the total group may or may not follow the symposium. Normally one does not expect to find conflict among the papers a routine aspect as, for example, is true of a panel or debate. Often the presentations are written. The method tends to be more formal and structured than, for example, a panel. Different resource persons may deal with only one aspect of the problem, topic or concept.

Techniques to Expedite Discussion

The following are not methods but techniques used by meeting planners to facilitate discussion. Some are variations of learning methods already discussed. They are included here to indicate the endless variety of meeting techniques.

Conpar Technique. Primarily, the ingredient introduced in the conpar technique is a timekeeper and a buzzer to control the time allotted to panel members, speakers or forum members. This specific technique is more complicated, but a detailed explanation is not necessary. Many similar techniques involving chimes, flags, hand signals, lights, bells, gongs, guns and other devices to give resource persons or audience responders or questioners a warning some 30 seconds before their allotted time is up and a loud warning when they have used all their time are employed. Some would appear useful or desirable for a change of pace. Others would seem to focus on the device employed and detract from the content. As is so often true, any device that will facilitate accomplishment of objectives is desirable. Too often the device utilized is so novel, so obtrusive or so horse-playish that it cancels out its basic purpose.

Brain-Storming. In a brain-storming session—well known technique—a problem is posed by a leader. One or more recorders jot down ideas as fast as the group calls them out. The idea is to get "way out" ideas; participants can express their ideas, and no explanations are offered. Later, judgment is applied to the ideas recorded.

Buzzboard. A board—buzzboard—in front of the audience has numbers corresponding to numbers on the group tables. When a table has a question or comment, it presses a button which lights up its number on the buzzboard, and the group is recognized.

Check Lists. Check lists of all kinds are employed to test knowledge or how a group feels about the subject matter or a part of the subject matter.

Circular Response. In the circular response method, anyone in a group begins by making a comment on whatever subject the group is to discuss. The next person on his right adds to this comment or makes a comment of his own. This continues until everyone has spoken. No one can speak a second time until all members of the group have been heard from once.

Movie Forum. Two films or video tapes, representing opposite or conflicting sides of an issue, are presented in the movie forum. The film episodes or speakers take the place of live speakers. It may be used in the context of a debate or panel.

One Question Technique. Following a presentation, the audience is divided into small informal groups to discuss the content and formulate individual questions. Each small group may write out one question it wants dealt with by the resource person.

Quiz. Tests are often used to test knowledge or to stimulate discussion.

Read-Around Technique. When discussing written material (for example, a policy), one group member should read a paragraph and then explain in his own words what he understands it to mean. If the group does not agree, it is discussed until there is agreement. The next participant then reads a paragraph, and the process is repeated.

Room-Hopping. Topics are set up for different tables in the room-hopping method. Signs on the table announce the topic. Participants sit in on the discussion at that table until they feel they have learned what they wanted to learn. They then move to another table.

Skit. Less formal and shorter than a play, skits are best when written by a knowledgeable, talented person. They are concise and to the point and can present problems in a humorous way. They are most often used to show conflict or "how not to. . ."

Slip Technique. Each group member takes a 3- by 5-inch card in the slip technique and writes out a question, thought or idea he has on the subject the group is to discuss. The cards are collected and exchanged with a different group. This gives more insight into the subject than is possible, normally, with the members of a single group.

Tables of Information. A knowledgeable resource person is assigned a subject matter for tables of information. The subject title is placed on a table sign. Discussions continue for 30 minutes, with the resource person assigned to that table. At a given signal, participants can move to another table. Not more than three such half-hour sessions should be scheduled. This method is known by many names—for example, "Cracker Barrel."

One of the questions that will occur to the meeting planner is, "How can I use this information about groupings, methods and techniques?" Once the meeting planner knows his major meeting objectives and content, he must then determine the best groupings

Table 4.1. Groupings and Methods to Use to Accomplish Objectives

Meeting Objectives	Groupings to Use	Methods to Use
Impart information	Orientation Special interest Large audience	Reading; programmed instruction; consulting teams; case study; colloquy; confrontation; demonstration; debate; exercise; field trip; forum; lecture; filmed involvement; panel; project; symposium
Develop a manual skill	Application Occupational Skill practice Drill	Consulting teams; demonstration; drill and practice; exercise; gaming; guided experience; in-basket
Exchange experiences	Application Buzz Occupational Phillips 66	Reading; programmed instruction; consulting team; neighbor discussion; case study; field trip; forum; in-basket; incident process; lecture; panel; role play; symposium
Change behavior	Application Diagnostic Skill practice Special interest	Reflection; consulting team; confrontation; drill and practice; encounter; exercise; gaming; laboratory; marathon; role play; sensitivity
Solve a problem	Application	Programmed instruction; reflection; consulting team; case study; colloquy; confrontation; demonstration; exercise; field trip; gaming; incident process; problem-solving; project; role play

and methods to attain the objectives. The matrix in Table 4.1 is one way this can be approached. The grouping and methods listed opposite each objective are not exhaustive or rank-ordered. It can be debated whether some have been included which should not have been, and vice versa.

It is necessary always to aim
    at being interesting rather than exact,
for the spectator forgives everything
    except dreariness.

Voltaire

5
Audio-Visual
Aids

It is not the intent of this book to present an exhaustive treatment of audio-visual aids. The various methods of transparency preparation, explanation of the physics and optics involved, costs, varieties available and techniques for effective use are the proper subject of a separate book. Listing the more common aids available, suggesting the more common traps to avoid and listing some reference material that is commonly needed but hard to obtain will be covered.

The first thing to emphasize is that an aid is just that—it is not designed to be the message itself—but often is. If an aid will assist in getting a message across, its use should normally be considered. The meeting planner is then presented with the problem of selecting the proper aid. If the aid draws attention to itself, it is not functional. Aids can be so elaborate or gimmicky that the real message is obscured. Similarly, no aid can substitute for a point or

Figure 5.1. Cautions in using audio-visual aids.

1. When using projected material, the meeting planner should be sure the lettering can be read. It is appalling how many visuals still use type or lettering unreadable past 10 feet.
2. Visuals should be relatively uncluttered. The object is not to see how much can be placed on a visual but to feature a cardinal point or two.
3. When a choice must be made between a well-done simple visual or a shabby elaborate visual, the well-done should always be chosen.
4. When using film, video tape and similar aids, the meeting planner should have a qualified operator. A poorly projected sound or visual aid detracts significantly from the session, and the toll on materials is devasting.
5. The aid should be checked in advance to be sure it is working. Spare critical parts, such as lamps, should be on hand. The planner should check to see if an extension cord or three-way plug adapter is needed. Sometimes obvious things are overlooked, like the projector being on the same circuit as the room lights—turn out the room lights and the projector goes off.
6. A good aid should not be worked to death. The planner must avoid being a "Well, we can always show a film" meeting planner.
7. The planner should be sure everyone can see the aid—and that the aid is large enough to be seen. The aid is useless when the resource person has to say, "This is a swell visual; I wish those of you beyond the third row could see it."

8. Aids must be kept updated. The sight of scratches, dog-ears or a calendar in a visual showing a year a decade ago indicates to the participant that the presentation idea is not exactly "with it."
9. The screen must be high enough for all to see. Also concern must be shown for those behind pillars, close down front and at the extreme sides.
10. Space for the projector or other aid and the operator must be provided.
11. Humor and cartoons must be watched. It is amazing how what seems so funny to the idea initiator, or at the moment the aid is developed, can seem so inappropriate when the aid is used.

message. Saying something trivial with the help of an effective aid only more dramatically points out the lack of a valid or significant message.

Most aids require advance preparation, which tends to give the message a "canned" feel. This is a subtle but real point. If the aid is obviously old and dated, it only adds to the impression that the message is not too relevant. If the content of the meeting sessions demands an aura of flexibility, immediate relevancy and spontaneity, then an aid may be dysfunctional. For this reason, for example, many resource persons dealing with changing attitudes and behavior and using "here and now" data will not use most audio-visual aids. The major exception would be aids such as blackboards and newsprint pads. On the other hand, some of the conceptual presentations and materials in such meetings could benefit significantly by using well-selected and well-prepared aids.

There are some general cautions that should be mentioned. Any meeting planner needs only to attend a few meetings to realize how frequently the most obvious mistakes are repeated over and over. General cautions are listed in Figure 5.1.

Figure 5.2. Audio aids.

---

1. Tape recorder, including cassettes
2. Record player
3. Teaching machines using audio
4. Public address systems (including floor and table microphones)
5. Radio
6. Telephone
7. Buzzers of all kinds

Aids have been divided into three categories: audio aids (Figure 5.2), visual aids (Figure 5.3) and audio-visual aids (Figure 5.4). The listing is not exhaustive but does encompass the most frequently used ones. No attempt has been made to describe them, to explain how they work or are constructed or to define them. The listings are included here mostly as a reminder and check list for the meeting planner.

Sometimes interesting and novel variations can be made of a large aid. For example, small flip charts, about 4 or 5 inches can be prepared and given to each participant. They follow the presentation using the small flip chart before them—set up on their table.

The visuals in Figure 5.3 are all two-dimensional. Some visuals are three-dimensional. These include actual item, demonstration when it is wordless, mock-up and model.

From time to time the meeting planner needs some limited technical data as he constructs or uses audio-visual aids. The reference material in Figures 5.5 through 5.9 and in Table 5.1 is the data most frequently needed.

Figure 5.3. Visual aids.

1. One-way mirrors
2. Blackboard
3. Flip chart (material prepared in advance and "flipped")
4. Newsprint pads and easel (sometimes also called flip charts)
5. Flannel board
6. Magnetic board
7. Overhead transparency projector
8. Opaque projector
9. Films without sound
10. Slide projector (most common is the 2- by 2-inch and the 3½- by 4-inch)
11. Chart
12. Map
13. Diagram
14. Graph (bar, pie, line, picto)
15. Picture
16. Cork board/bulletin board
17. Poster
18. Photographs
19. Programmed instruction texts
20. Cutouts
21. Books
22. Articles
23. Outlines
24. Workbooks
25. Instruction sheets
26. Manuals
27. Shadow graphs
28. Speaker prompters
29. "Accordion" pull-out displays
30. Displays
31. Drawings
32. Special lighting effects—as psychodelic lighting
33. Instruments such as quizzes
34. Schematics
35. Fluorescents—such as chalk and paint
36. Venetian blind effect

Figure 5.4. Audio-visual aids.

1. Tape recorder with slides
2. Records with slides
3. Video tape
4. Television
5. Motion pictures with sound (either front view or rear view projected)
6. Puppets and puppet shows
7. Demonstrations with words
8. Field trip

Figure 5.5. Color combinations: descending order of most pleasing and effective combinations (courtesy of 3M Company, Visual Products Division).

1. Black on yellow
2. Black on orange
3. Orange on navy blue
4. Green on white
5. Scarlet-red on white
6. Black on white
7. Navy blue on white
8. White on navy blue
9. Orange on black
10. White on black
11. White on battle-green
12. White on scarlet-red
13. White on purple
14. Purple on white
15. Navy blue on yellow
16. Navy blue on orange
17. Yellow on black
18. Scarlet-red on yellow
19. Yellow on navy blue
20. Purple on yellow

Figure 5.6. Template for minimum image size (courtesy of 3M Company, Business Products Center).

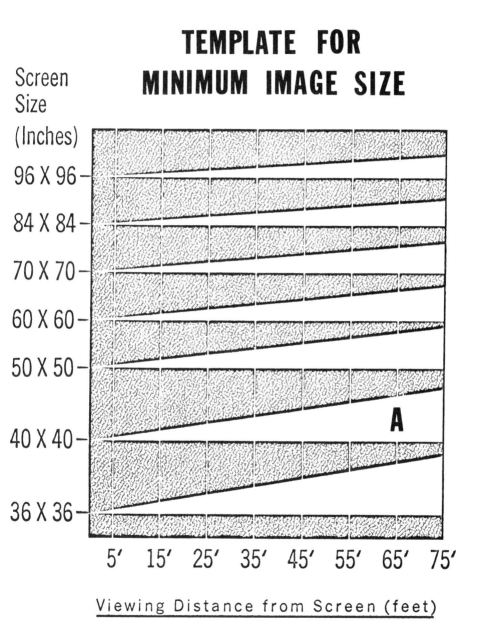

TEMPLATE FOR
MINIMUM IMAGE SIZE

Screen Size (Inches)

96 X 96

84 X 84

70 X 70

60 X 60

50 X 50

40 X 40

36 X 36

A

5'   15'   25'   35'   45'   55'   65'   75'

Viewing Distance from Screen (feet)

Figure 5.7. Preparation of transparency originals (courtesy of 3M Company, Business Products Center).

1. Typing
   a. Capital Letters on Pica Typewriter Absolute Minimum Size
   b. Speech or Primer Typewriter Size Most Readable (Note: Check typewriter ribbon to make sure typing can be copied)
2. Hand lettering
   a. Plastic Lettering Guide-for Slant or Block Type
   b. Professional Lettering Kits
   c. Free Hand
      1. Use No. 2 Lead Pencil (reproduces best on copying machine)
      2. Use Black Ink (cannot be corrected)
3. Professional lettering or printing
   a. Most Effective for Large Meeting
   b. Professional Looking
   c. Black Reproduces Best
   (Note: Copy should have at least one-inch margins. Projector stage is 10 x 10 inches.)

Selecting a Lens for the Desired Image Size and Projection Distance*

The size of the screen image should be selected so that all necessary detail is clearly visible from the longest viewing distance. The minimum size of the square screen can be determined by

*These suggestions and table were supplied courtesy of E. Leitz, Inc., Rockleigh, New Jersey.

Figure 5.8. Projection chart for VU-graph (courtesy of Technifax Corporation, Holyoke, Massachusetts).

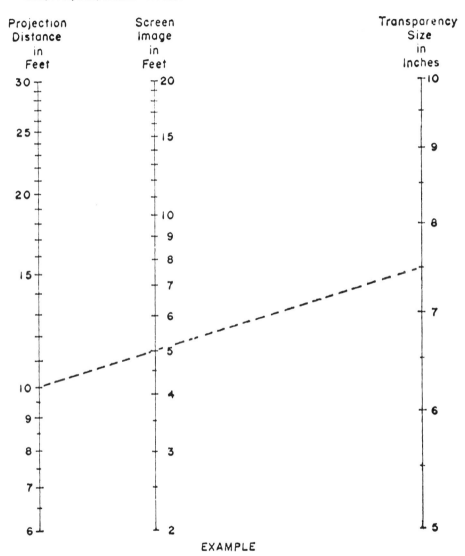

EXAMPLE

Given: Projection Distance 10 feet, Transparency 7.5" square
Find   Screen Image Size 5'x5'

Note: If transparency is rectangular in shape, make two readings, one for height, one for width.

Figure 5.9. Minimum height of lettering for the VU-graph (courtesy of Technifax Corporation, Holyoke, Massachusetts).

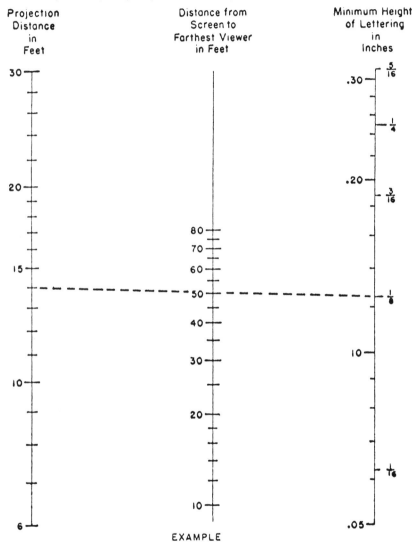

EXAMPLE

Given: Projection Distance, 14 Feet
Distance from Screen to Farthest Viewer, 50 Feet
Find: Minimum Height of Lettering .125", or $\frac{1}{8}$"

Table 5-1

	TRANSPARENCIES 24×36 mm											TRANSPARENCIES 2¼ x 2¼" or 2¾ x 2¾" (effective size 54×54 mm)				
	FOCAL LENGTH OF PROJECTION LENSES IN mm															
PROJECTION DISTANCES IN FEET	35	50	85	90	100	120	150	175	200	250	300	150	175	200	250	300
7'	6'7"	4'9"														
10'	9'10"	7'1"	4'	3'9"	3'5"							3'5"				
13'	13'1"	9'2"	5'3"	5'1"	4'7"	3'11"						4'7"	4'1"	3'5"		
16'		11'6"	6'7"	6'6"	5'11"	4'11"	3'11"					5'9"	5'1"	4'3"	3'5"	
20'		13'9"	8'2"	7'8"	7'1"	5'11"	4'7"	4'3"				7'1"	6'1"	5'3"	4'1"	3'7"
23'			9'4"	9'	8'3"	6'11"	5'5"	4'9"				8'2"	7'1"	6'1"	4'9"	4'1"
26'			10'8"	10'4"	9'4"	7'8"	6'3"	5'5"	4'7"			9'4"	8'	6'11"	5'7"	4'9"
30'			12'3"	11'6"	10'6"	8'10"	7'1"	6'1"	5'3"			10'6"	9'2"	7'10"	6'3"	5'3"
33'			13'6"	12'10"	11'8"	9'10"	7'10"	6'11"	5'9"	4'7"		11'8"	10'2"	8'8"	6'11"	5'11"
36'					12'11"	10'10"	8'6"	7'5"	6'5"	5'1"		12'11"	11'4"	9'6"	7'7"	6'7"
39'					14'1"	11'10"	9'4"	8'2"	6'11"	5'7"	4'7"	14'1"	12'4"	10'6"	8'4"	7'1"
43'						12'10"	10'2"	8'10"	7'7"	6'1"	4'11"		13'1"	11'6"	9'	7'9"
46'						13'9"	11'	9'6"	8'2"	6'7"	5'5"		14'1"	12'4"	9'10"	8'2"
49'							11'8"	9'10"	8'8"	7'1"	5'9"			13'1"	10'6"	8'10"
52'							12'2"	10'8"	9'4"	7'5"	6'1"			14'1"	11'2"	9'6"
56'								11'6"	9'10"	7'10"	6'7"				11'10"	10'
59'								12'4"	10'6"	8'4"	6'11"				12'8"	10'8"
62'								13'1"	11'2"	8'10"	7'3"				13'3"	11'4"
66'								13'9"	11'10"	9'4"	7'9"				14'1"	11'10"
69'									12'4"	9'10"	8'					12'4"
72'									12'10"	10'4"	8'4"					13'
82'									14'9"	11'10"	9'6"					14'9"
98'										14'1"	11'6"					
115'											13'5"					

Note (printed in the left-center region of the table): Figures give the longer screen image side. Corresponding square projection screens should be used to allow for horizontal and vertical pictures of the 24 x 36 mm frame

measurement of the distance between the screen and the back row of seats and dividing the result by 6.

Example: The back row is 54 feet from the screen. Dividing by 6 we obtain 9, so that the screen in this case must measure at least 9 by 9 feet.

Table 5.1 indicates the projection distance and the side length of the square screen required for the different lens focal lengths.

By experience we find out a short way
   for a long wandering;
learning teaches more in one year
   than experience in twenty.

Roger Ascham (1515-68) The Scholemaster

6
Physical
Arrangements

Form and mechanics do not make a meeting. If a group really wants to work and if the problem or need that brings them to a meeting is real and is so perceived by them, the meeting planner can be assured the group will work effectively even under adverse conditions. All that physical aspects can do is to make it possible for the group to work more effectively toward achieving their objective. Few meeting objectives, however, are seen by participants as being highly central in their lives. For that reason, and because physical facilities can significantly contribute to meeting objectives, careful attention to the physical arrangements is very important.

Experienced meeting planners have learned the importance of covering every detail and making specific assignments. It is a good idea to have a written confirmation of actions taken and to see that this is shared with all persons who need to know. The rationale for this is quickly seen if a strategic person becomes suddenly ill or is transferred. Generally for small meetings, it is not effective to depend upon much committee responsibility. The problem of communications is very difficult, and the meeting planner will find, if he fragments responsibility too much, that the meeting is the victim of conflicting arrangements and of critical jobs left undone.

If responsibility must be delegated to local groups at some physical distance, particular care must be taken for it is amazing the misunderstandings that can occur. Overhead transparency projectors are confused with opaque projectors or slide projectors. Local groups tend to be overly cost conscious and will book an important meeting in the basement of an old courthouse storage room to save money. Often others are blocked by thinking only of classroom style seating. A meeting depending upon much use of small groups is booked into a room 10 by 15 feet—for 50 participants. The planner or assistant at the other end must be knowledgeable of training methodology and group needs. If at all possible, the planner should physically visit and see the meeting facility.

Meeting Dates

One of the most frequently overlooked considerations is the date for the meeting. Some meeting purposes require a specific date, regardless of other considerations. Generally, however, the meeting planners have some control over the dates. Several years ago there was a general assumption that meetings could not be scheduled during July and August because people were on vacations. This is changing; winter vacations have become rather popular. More and more organizations are finding they can schedule meetings during the summer. Other considerations that must be weighed are listed in Figure 6.1.

The Meeting Facility

Having checked the factors listed in Figure 6.1 and determining a date for the meeting, the meeting planner is now ready to

Figure 6.1. Points to consider in choosing a meeting date.

1. Does the objective of the meeting dictate specific dates?
2. What about weather? A resort that looks great in July may look quite different in January, even if the rates are attractive.
3. What are the off-peak times for the meeting facility?
   a. If the meeting can fit into the facility's slack periods, often better rates, better rooms and better service can be obtained for less money.
   b. Most facilities, but not all, are underbooked during Christmas, Easter, Memorial Day week, Fourth of July, Labor Day and Thanksgiving.
   c. Sometimes local observances will add to the list.
   d. The most demand for facilities seems to be September, October, November, March, April and May.
   e. Weekends generally tend to be underbooked.
4. Holidays—attention should not only be focused on national holidays but also on local and regional observances and on the religious holidays of the participants.
5. Sometimes organizational history and tradition cannot be ignored: "We always have this meeting the last week in October." Frequently the plans of participants and their families are built around this date.
6. Operational business and relative slackness in the organization conducting the meeting should be considered.
7. Other meeting demands for participants should not be disregarded. Often the meeting will conflict with other professional meetings scheduled far in advance.
8. Other meetings scheduled by other parts of the organization should not be overlooked.

look for a facility. It should be kept in mind that a facility for a relatively small meeting is the subject of concern here—not a large facility and satellite requirements as are needed by a convention. It is also assumed that an elaborate meeting committee structure is not needed. The steps for planning a small meeting are much the same as required for a large meeting, and many of the requirements are the same. However, responsibility is centered in a very small group, and committee organization is generally not needed—or a very simple structure is needed. For that reason, typical committees and their assignments will not be discussed. These include facilities, finance, registration, entertainment, international guests, transportation, evaluation, hotel reservations, speakers, banquet, hospitality, program, exhibit and administrative committees.

Usually the small meeting planner will be concerned with requirements for a large meeting room to accommodate up to 100 participants; small meeting rooms or facilities to accommodate six to 10 small groups of about 10 members to a group, audio-visual aids, meals, coffee breaks, rooms, parking and transportation, duplicating services; and sometimes a small room for a secretary or administrative assistant. These are the most important items to check out.

Location. Is the facility easily reached from the airport or by driving? What limousine service is available and at what hours? How does this mesh with public transportation schedules? How far from downtown (participants may wish to "get away" in the evening)?

Parking. Is it adequate and protected?

Facility. Is it relatively new and modern? Clean? Staff competent and adequate? The layout functional to meeting's purposes?

Sundries. Can participants easily get newspapers, toilet articles, simple health articles, haircuts, laundry and dry cleaning?

Transportation. Can people get there reasonably easy? Often opening and closing sessions pay no attention to transportation realities, with the result that the opening and closing sessions are only half attended, and many unkind things are said about the meeting planning.

Medical assistance. What happens if a participant gets ill? Is a doctor on call or available? Illness to participants happens more frequently than most meeting planners realize.

Rooms. What is the cost? Any discounts? Can the facility supply the number of singles you require? What is check-out time? Will they make the reservations for participants? What is the procedure?

Facilities for wives. If wives and families will attend, are they isolated or can they go on their own?

Meeting rooms. These should be looked at as well as what surrounds them. The planner should not be trapped by seeing it in off-periods. What activities will envelop participants during the meeting? The planner should look for things like adjacent kitchens, heavy traffic inside and outside, construction work inside and outside. He should check if the rooms are his for the duration of the meeting, or are other meetings scheduled in the rooms? It is extremely annoying and nonfunctional to "pack up" materials each evening and to require participants to "clear their spaces." Are there columns to block the view? Is the ceiling high enough for a screen? Is the room suitable for table and chair plans. Small meeting rooms should be looked at with the same kind of questions in mind. What kinds of tables and chairs will be supplied? Rooms using folding doors or screens should be considered with care; these are almost always unsatisfactory.

Meals and breaks. Are coffee and soft drinks to be served? How much? Where? Can times be changed? Keep in mind that most participants would prefer to eat on their own. If group meals are to be served, the menu should be examined—better yet, the food should be tasted. How are gratuities handled? Where will the coffee and cokes be served? Is there room?

Duplicating facilities. If duplicating facilities are to be used, what kind of resources are available? How much lead time must be given? What is the cost?

Audio-visual equipment. Needs should be known by now. Does the facility have them? The equipment should be examined.

Will it be available when needed? What is the cost? Is the facility in a location that requires the employment of equipment operators even if the planner can operate the equipment himself? Where are the electrical outlets? Can the room be darkened? What of mike outlets?

Tables and chairs. What are available? How does this fit into the plans? Is the number of tables and chairs sufficient?

Phones, message handling, washrooms. Requirements must be met.

Personnel. The meeting planner should know with whom he will be working and try to meet them. These people are critical to the meeting planner because contacts will not be with the manager or program manager but with the head waiter, waitress who handles breaks, electrician, engineer and the porters who handle the room setups. Are they knowledgeable?

Plans. Does the facility want meeting plans in writing? The room layouts? The meeting schedules? Does the facility have its own forms? Who should get the information?

Early setup. It is highly desirable to set the meeting room(s) up the night before the meeting opens. If materials are missing, they can still be secured, or substitutes can be found. Trying to set the room up the same morning the meeting opens is often awkward because of the early arrival of some participants. It is good to look, and be, prepared.

Can the room be entered the evening before for an early setup? If materials are to be shipped to the facility, can they be removed? Will porter help be available? Will the room be set up as requested in layout requests? Often the room will be booked for another meeting the night before—or locked—or materials not available—or help unavailable—etc. The meeting planner should make certain that his planning can be implemented.

Registration facilities. Is space available? Is equipment needed for registration available? Can materials be placed in mailboxes in advance?

Exhibits. If exhibits are used, where is the area? It should be examined. What is the cost? What are the put-up and takedown times? What costs are involved?

Hospitality suite. Do plans include a general room for drinks, relaxation and informality? If so, where will it be located? Will the hotel provide it free? If not, what is the cost? What is the limitation on liquor in the room? What are the arrangements for card tables, cards, etc?

After the facility has been decided, the next step is to ask—if they are needed for participants—for brochures describing the facility and directions for reaching it. Understandings with the facility should be put in writing and sent to the facility, and written confirmation should be requested.

Attention will now be focused on some of the more specific elements, related to physical arrangements, with which the meeting planner will need to concern himself.

Announcing the Meeting

Most meeting participants have numerous demands on their time. The meeting should be announced well in advance—how far will depend upon factors like urgency of the meeting, calendars of the participants, availability of a suitable facility, etc. Normally a minimum of two months notice is desirable. If the first notice exceeds two months, at least one, and possibly two, reminders may be desirable. Even a notice of one to two months needs a reminder follow-up about one week before the meeting.

Participants should receive an agenda. They should know what advance preparation they need to make, whether and how they make hotel reservations, room and other costs, plans for registration, information about suitable dress, times of the opening and closing sessions, directions for travel, date of meeting, materials they need to bring, an indication of who is being invited, and some information as to who the resource persons will be and the methodology to be employed.

Registration

Location for registration must be known, and arrangements for it to be well marked and identified should be made. The meeting planner should know who will staff it during what hours. Staffers must be knowledgeable about the program, the facility and the community. What is to be distributed, what forms are to be filled out and what records are to be kept—all this must be specified. If money is collected, the desk must have ample small bills and change. Staffers must be informed whom to call when they get pertinent questions they cannot answer—and where that person can be reached at all times. They must know the facility layout and the layout of the meeting rooms. If special arrangements apply to resource persons, this should be made specific. For example, will resource persons receive complimentary meal tickets?

The staff at the registration desk is a key staff—whether this be one or more persons. Often this is the participant's first contact with the meeting, and the impression made can be critical. Too often the meeting planner sees this function as "garbage" and assigns it a low priority, and the service and organization rises to the description.

Meeting Rooms

The check list in Figure 6.2 is useful as a reminder. Not all the points listed are applicable to all meeting purposes.

Figure 6.2. Considerations to weigh in selecting meeting rooms.

1. Generally it is better to use a room that is rectangular.
2. Rooms with internal columns should be avoided, if possible.
3. It is best to use exit doors at the back of the room so latecomers will not interrupt the meeting.

(Figure 6.2 continued on following page)

(Figure 6.2 continued below and on following page)

4. Chairs located so participants face open windows or other glaring light sources should be avoided.

5. If more than 25 participants will use the room, a raised platform of 6 to 12 inches for the resource persons might be used.

6. The meeting planner should make sure the power source for visual projectors is not on the same circuit as the room lights.

7. He should experiment with where the resource persons should work. Often facility custom prevails when another arrangement might be more functional.

8. He should check ventilation and heat controls.

9. He should look for noise sources and do what can be done to eliminate or to reduce them.

10. He should check for phones in the room or nearby. He may want to arrange with the facility to disconnect or not to ring them during the meeting sessions.

11. Is there a place to post messages and phone calls?

12. If coffee and soft drink breaks are to occur in the room, where can space be arranged so it is adequate and as unobtrusive as possible?

13. Will a table for resource materials or for a library be needed? Where should it be located?

14. If small groups will use the large meeting room, where will they meet? What chairs will they use? Will screens be needed?

15. If the meeting room is adjacent to other meeting rooms to be used by other groups, special pains should be taken to be sure when they will be used and the type of activity. No folding screen can block off the noise of a sound film or public-address system being used in the room next door.

16. Are signs needed to identify the small meeting rooms?

17. Will ashtrays, water glasses, water pitchers and waste baskets be available?
18. If visuals are to be used, can the windows be darkened? Can all lights be turned off? Where are the switches (it is surprising how many times they are in another room or in a locked closet)?
19. What are the facilities for checking coats and hats?
20. Can ample aisle space and space around the perimeter of the room be provided?

Materials and Meeting Aids

It is apparent that not all of the items listed in Figure 6.3 are appropriate for all meetings. Again, what is appropriate depends upon the type of meeting, the methodology used, the number of

Figure 6.3. Materials and meeting aids.

1. Name cards or name tents
   a. Prepared in advance or to be prepared by participants?
   b. If prepared by participants, felt pens in sufficient quantity must be available.
2. Signs outside meeting rooms to identify them
3. Tablets or other note-taking means
4. Pencils—sharpened
5. Pencil sharpener
6. Three-hole punch
7. Paper clips
8. Masking tape
9. Transparency tape

(Figure 6.3 continued on following page)

(Figure 6.3 continued)

10. Wrapping materials if participants' materials are to be shipped for them
11. Water pitchers
12. Glasses
13. Ashtrays
14. Participants' notebooks
15. Advance reading materials
16. Library or other resource table
17. Handouts to be distributed
18. Are materials to be reproduced? If so, are the equipment, supplies and operator available?
19. Flag or banners
20. Agendas or programs
21. Roster of participants
22. Rubber bands
23. Lapel badges
24. Stapler and staples
25. Staple remover
26. Ruler
27. Scissors
28. Small hammer
29. Medium sized screwdriver
30. Pliers
31. Bulletin board
32. Typewriter
33. Simple first aid equipment: aspirin, small adhesive bandages, etc.

participants, the length of the meeting, etc. However, the meeting planner will find this, or a similar, check list useful as a reminder and sometimes to suggest an aid not normally considered.

Audio-Visual Aids

The variety of audio-visual aids available was discussed in an earlier chapter. No attempt is made here to deal with these individually, except for the most commonly employed aids. Figure 6.4 lists only the most commonly overlooked items related to audio-visual aids of all kinds.

Figure 6.4. Audio-visual aids.

1. Usually the meeting planner will use a blackboard or newsprint paper and easel. If a blackboard is used, ample chalk and an eraser must be on hand. The blackboard should be checked in advance—an unusually odd assortment of objects receive this name by facilities. If newsprint and easels are used, the planner must be sure the paper is of the right size, that the easel has solid back for writing, that ample felt pens or other writing instruments are available, that pads and easels are available in the small meeting rooms and that facilities are available for hanging the pad sheets when small groups report. For this purpose, masking tape, thumb tacks and magnetic strips around the room are used.
2. If a public address system is used, the planner must know how it works and where the controls are located. If floor mikes are used, he should check in advance to see how many are available, where they can be located and the maximum number that can be set up in the room.
3. For equipment like projectors, he should be positive the room lights and the electrical outlet for the projector are not on the same system.
4. Can the room be darkened?

(Figure 6.4 continued on following page)

(Figure 6.4 continued)

5. Is the ceiling high enough to raise a screen to viewing height?
6. Is a qualified projectionist available? Can he make simple repairs or bulb replacements?
7. Film or other visuals should be checked in advance to be sure they are in proper sequence, rewound, not broken and the right item (film, for example, has a way of being in the wrong container).
8. Extra light and sound lamps should be on hand.
9. A screen large enough for projected picture to be seen by all participants must be secured.
10. Extension cord should be available.
11. Adapter for three-prong plugs to fit two-prong wall receptacle should be secured.
12. Acetate rolls and writing pencils for overhead transparency projector must be available.
13. Speaker's table and lectern must be set up.
14. Light for speakers table should be secured.
15. Gavel can be used.
16. Pointer can be made available.
17. Location of all room light switches and wall electrical outlets should be known, and the voltage should be checked.
18. If material must be rented, who is the supplier? What is the charge? Must an operator be taken with the equipment?
19. Can people see and hear?
20. Examine—check—try out—do not assume all is in working condition and ready to go. *Know* it is ready.

Speaker or Resource Person Arrangements

Few arrangements are handled more poorly than working with the resource persons or speakers. The resource person should be tailored to the needs of the meeting; so often a meeting planner secures the resource person and then designs the meeting around his availability and capability. Good resource persons are in demand; selection should be made as early as possible and the selected person contacted.

Requirements of the meeting and group should be outlined. The resource person, if necessary, should be asked if he has the interest and capability for the job—does he feel comfortable? Part of the answer as to whether he feels comfortable with the content and meeting purposes will depend upon the fee, if any. It is simply amazing how more comfortable one can get with an assignment as the fee goes up. The honorarium must be stated and whether this includes travel and other expenses. If an agreement is reached, the arrangements should be confirmed in writing: time, date, place, topic, honorarium.

Determine when he will arrive. Is he to be met? When will the planner get together with him? Where? Does he need a room reservation? When? Who will make it? He must be given directions for reaching the facility.

By all means his address for mailing purposes and phone number must be secured. If he is on the road a good deal, who knows how to reach him?

Generally the poorest planning occurs in the briefing of resource persons. If the budget will permit, it is extremely useful for him to meet with a planning and steering committee, if used, or with the meeting planners. If this is not possible, he should be briefed fully on meeting objectives and purposes, the kinds of participants expected, their expectations, what will precede and follow him and expectations for what his session(s) will contribute to the meeting. If critical issues are involved—high sensitivity to something or unusually obstreperous persons are apt to evidence themselves—he should be informed. Most resource persons are highly motivated, and if they know meeting needs, they will exert a lot of initiative and preparation to meeting specific objectives. Too often he is simply asked, "What's your favorite talk this year?" If he shows unwillingness to prepare, nothing is lost—he was not the person for the meeting purposes.

A second check on the resource person a few days before the meeting is recommended. It is not impossible for correspondence to get lost, the wrong date to be entered in an appointment book or the resource person to forget to look at his appointment book.

A biographical sheet on the resource person should be obtained. The meeting planner should find out how best to introduce him to the group. His bio sheet might be included in the participants' workbook, and briefer introduction might be given.

The resource person needs to know the number of participants attending. If he is using handout materials, an agreement should be reached on how many copies are required and who will reproduce or supply them. If any costs are involved, who will pay for them?

The methodology to be employed, the exact times for his sessions and any involvement he will want from others should be arranged. For example, if he uses role plays or exercises, will he need an assistant or two? How are questions and discussions to be handled?

Normally in small meetings the meeting planner is not concerned with a photographer or the press. However, this is sometimes involved. If so, proper arrangements should be made, and the resource person must know these arrangements in advance as well as the kinds of questions he will probably be asked. He should also know the purposes to which the pictures and stories are to be put.

An increasingly pertinent question has recently arisen over the video-taping of the resource person, tape recording of his session, etc. For many resource persons this is becoming a delicate question. His career often depends upon his materials and concepts. If filming or taping, even by individuals, is apt to occur, this must be cleared in advance with the resource person. He may ask for a written clearance that the materials taped or recorded will only be used for individuals in the organization. Most resource persons would prefer the question not arise. If it is apt to occur, the question should be brought out in the open and a decision reached before the meeting. Proper announcements about the procedures or limitations can be made at the session.

Special Social Events

Most small meetings do not get involved in multiple and complex special and social events. Generally these are limited to field trips, receptions or cocktail parties.

The major caution regarding field trips is that they be planned for and sufficient time made available. Often they are spontaneous and poorly handled. Too frequently transportation is an afterthought. It takes time to get to the place being visited and time to do or see whatever is to be done or seen. If it is worth the effort, it is worth planning and not, "We'll see if we can't work something out after we close at 4:30 and before the cocktail party at 5:00."

If evening meetings are scheduled after a cocktail party, the session should not exceed 90 minutes, and participant involvement is a must. Drinking and night activities are accepted as part of the compensation of attending meetings—but the toll the next day can be considerable in fatigue.

Meals

Small meetings usually do not involve elaborate banquets or meals. If it can be done, most participants prefer eating on their own in small groups. Many participants skip lunch entirely, while many others have peculiar eating preferences. If group meals must be scheduled, the planner should try to get the facility to offer at least two entrées, one of which is quite light.

Figure 6.5. Post-meeting matters.

1. Meeting rooms must be cleared of all organizational or borrowed equipment and materials; he must also arrange for its return.
2. If reports or other items were promised to participants, action must be initiated to speed the items on their way.
3. Facility management must be contacted to assure all bills are in order and the facility understands who is to be billed.
4. Resource persons must be paid.
5. Was there a sponsor of the meeting who expects a report? If so, the report should be dictated while the meeting is still fresh in mind.
6. Do any letters of appreciation need to be sent?
7. Does a report need to be made for organizational records?

Post-Meeting Matters

After the meeting has been concluded, there is a real temptation for meeting planners to let up. They have worked hard and are tired. But, there are still some matters that need attention. These are listed in Figure 6.5.

We do not learn by inference and deduction
   and the application of mathematics to philosphy,
but by direct intercourse and sympathy.

H.D. Thoreau (1863) Excursions

7
Table and Chair
Constellations

The arrangement of tables and chairs in meeting rooms is far more complicated than answering the question most often asked, "How many can we crowd into this room?" Some, but not enough, study has explored the relationship of physical arrangements to meeting purpose. Some of these implications have been discussed in an earlier chapter, "Potpourri of Meeting Dynamics." This relationship has long been observed. For instance, Francis Bacon in "Of Counsel" commented long ago:

> The councils at this day in most places are but familiar meetings, where matters are rather talked on than debated; and they run too swift to the order or act of council. It were better that in causes of weight, the matter were propounded one day and not spoken to till the next day; "Night is the season for counsel", so was it done in the commission of union between England and Scotland, which was a grave and orderly

assembly. I commend set days for petitions; for both it gives the suitors more certainty for their attendance, and it frees the meetings for matters of estate, that they may "attend to the business in hand". In choice of committees for ripening business for the council, it is better to choose indifferent persons, than to make an indifferency by putting in those that are strong on both sides. I commend, also, standing commissions; as for trade, for treasure, for war, for suits, for some provinces; for where there be divers particular councils, and but one council of estate, they are in effect no more than standing commissions, save that they have greater authority. Let such as are to inform councils out of their particular professions (as lawyers, seamen, mint-men, and the like) be first heard before committees; and then, as occasion serve, before the council; for that is to clamor councils, not to inform them. A long table and a square table, or seats about the walls, seem things of form, but are things of substance; for at a long table a few at the upper end, in effect, sway all the business; but in the other form there is more use of the counsellors' opinions that sit lower. A king, when he presides in council, let him beware how he opens his own inclination too much in that which he propoundeth; for else counsellors will but take the wind of him, and, instead of giving free counsel, will sing him a song of "I shall please".

Meeting planners should understand that often they feel more comfortable with things tangible and with physical arrangements. However, when dealing with a dynamic process like a meeting, adjustability and adaptability cannot be fitted into any one point of time—for example, confining concern with it during the pre-planning time alone. Concern with adaptability must be evidenced throughout the meeting.

Basically, the arrangement of tables and chairs should be dictated by the kind of visual, auditory, internalization and interpersonal interactions expected of participants. People can hear when they cannot see; but, of course, they hear more accurately when they can see the speaker. If the major objective, for example, is to give information which can be received by auditory stimulation alone, the arrangement of the chairs should be dictated by the sound projection.

If the objective involves more than the giving of information, the program very likely will involve communication in a wide variety of patterns and the tables should be arranged to maximize the ability of each participant to see and hear all of the people with whom he is going to interact.

As simple as it may sound, the study of sound and light wave projection among the people who are expected to hear and see each other will suggest a wide variety of arrangements. Normally, the greater the extent of interaction, the smaller will be the groups and the more likely they will be located physically in a circular, rather than a rectangular, position.

The latter part of this chapter diagrams the most commonly used table and chair arrangements. It will be noted that they are related to the maximum trade-offs among factors like the projection of light waves, sound waves and degree of interaction and mental reflection desired.

Some other basic assumptions underlie the manipulation of the physical arrangements. For example:

1. Mutually supportive activity increases in probability as the size of the group decreases.
2. Heterogeneity is desirable in groups that need to develop new ideas.
3. Periodic changes in physical arrangements enhance the advantages of heterogeneity.

Other considerations will also influence the physical arrangements, such as:

1. People naturally talk less to others if there is difficulty in engaging them in direct line of sight. An example of this was mentioned earlier: participants often tend not to talk to persons seated by their side and do tend to talk to those seated opposite them.
2. Different positions have different symbolic values, but these symbolic values are not completely uniform for all persons. Nearness to a leader, for example, is a factor which many persons try to control in their selection of seating: some choosing positions opposite him in the apparent desire to compete.

3. The door to the meeting room is another significant location. People will range themselves with respect to the door, partly in symbolic expressions of their feeling of acceptance of the group and their desire either to identify with it or to escape from it.

Tables seem to be related to defense mechanisms. To many, a table represents a form of protection: a psychological sign: "I have something I can lean on—fend you off—hide under—etc." Tables in various settings support this observation. Physical arrangements vary from the very informal meeting setting, such as inviting several friends to one's home, to the most official of meeting purposes using structure such as is seen at a court trial. Many executives have found, for example, that the normal executive desk and chair and visitor's chair placement tends to make any interaction formal. To counteract this dynamic, many executives have taken larger office space that also includes a sofa, one or two soft chairs and a cocktail table. To enhance more informality and openness, the executive leaves his desk and chair and conducts the interview or meeting at the more informal setting of easy chairs, sofa and cocktail table. The various "talk shows" on television offer other examples of how the physical arrangements are manipulated to increase informality, openness and interaction.

A table can be, to the group and to the discussion or task, either a barrier or a support. It is a kind of semicommunication line. The contour of the table and chair arrangements often literally dictate the flow of communication. Meeting planners and participants have no name for this, it is a reality more "felt" than recognized openly. This dynamic can be, depending upon the circumstances, either a threat or a promise.

The meeting planner can capitalize on these dynamics. He will find that participants get a different feeling by sitting in a circle of chairs without tables than they do when a table is introduced in the same setting. When sitting around a round table, people need to lean forward a bit to see everyone else. Then, as one participant commented, "I say to myself, 'Since I've gone to this much effort, I might as well participate.'"

A meeting planner must understand that a meeting room, chairs and tables can be too plush, alluring or forbidding. A board room identified as such by the participants is not a good surrounding for informality, brainstorming, idea creation or innovation. The past uses and decisions emanating from the room, the massive stolidness and formality of the chairs and tables and the incessant glares of past organizational figures staring from paintings or photographs on the walls quite effectively bottle up interaction and creativity. Another example of this phenomenon has been noted by meeting planners when they conduct training activities on a university, college or other formal educational facility. Many comment that the participants seem to study, work and participate more intently—possibly influenced by the stimulus-response effect triggered from their past educational experiences. Similarly, meeting outdoors has limited usage—the opportunities for escape behavior are significantly increased. It is also well for the meeting planner to recognize that some degree of physical discomfort seems related to learning. Chairs can be too deep, too low and too comfortable.

The meeting planner must watch out, in seating people at tables, for too narrow a table, poor leader visibility, not seating groups in conflict across from each other and poor leader position. Participants should not be seated too closely together. Part of this relates to the phenomena of territorial imperative—individual space requirements. Part of it also relates to the fact that if chairs are placed at about arm's length from each other, side conversations are discouraged. Related to this are the phenomena of subgroups. To assist in preventing subgroup formation, groups of about six to eight persons seem best. When more than eight participants are placed in a group, there is a real tendency to lose intimacy and to encourage the formation of subgroups.

If meetings rooms are to be used repeatedly or if it is impossible to make "on the spot" observations and experimentations, a useful device is to chart out a scale model of the rooms. Scale models of chairs and tables are prepared and manipulated on the room model to experiment with the different table and chair

Figure 7.1. Some suggestions in arranging meeting rooms.

1. The minimum space between tables and the side of the room should be 3 feet.
2. The minimum space between tables and the ends of the room should be 5 feet. Ten feet for the resource person end of the room is preferred.
3. If participants are to be seated on both sides of a rectangular table, the table should be a minimum of 30 inches wide. Less than that and the employment of ashtrays, water glasses, notebooks and lack of room to write is most annoying.
4. A 5-foot table should accommodate, along each side, two participants; a 6-foot table, three participants; an 8-foot table, four participants.
5. Rectangular tables 18 inches wide are best for classroom style, where participants are to be seated on only one side of the table.
6. In classroom style, a minimum distance of 36 inches between rows of tables should be allowed.
7. If coffee breaks are to be in the room, a separate space that is adequate should be allowed.
8. When round tables are used, it is generally best not to set them up in rows but to stagger them. A minimum of 5 feet should be allowed between tables.
9. A round table of 4 feet should accommodate six participants; a 5-foot table, eight participants uncrowded or 10 participants somewhat crowded; and a 6-foot table should accommodate 10 participants uncrowded or 12 participants crowded. Larger round tables are sometimes employed; they are not too effective where a large number of tables are being used in the same room. The noise factor and difficulty of hearing

are significantly increased. They can, however, be used in separate meeting rooms with good effect.
10. A minimum of 30 inches should be allowed for each chair—36 inches is much better.
11. If it is necessary to seat people at tables back-to-back, allow at least 5 feet between tables—6 feet is better.

arrangements that can be accommodated in the room for the number of participants expected. A magnetic board is often useful for this purpose. One factor often overlooked is the height of the ceiling—particularly when a projector screen is to be used.

The best rectangular tables are 30 inches wide, 30 inches high and 5 or 6 feet long. It is desirable to have a few other lengths, the most useful being 4 and 8 feet. It is jeopardous to list guides, they can be suggestions only and may need to be changed depending upon meeting purpose, audio-visual limitations, sizes or rooms, tables and chairs available, etc. However, the list in Figure 7.1 is a useful guide.

The arrangement of tables and chairs is almost endless in variety. The basic designs of table arrangements have been arbitrarily divided into five broad categories:

1. Those using round tables or a circular or semicircular arrangement (Figures 7.2 through 7.8).
2. Those using a variation of a square (Figures 7.9 through 7.11)
3. Those using a variation of a rectangle (Figures 7.12 through 7.20)
4. Those employing the shape of a letter of the alphabet (Figures 7.21 through 7.31).
5. Those not falling into any one predominant category (Figures 7.32 through 7.34).

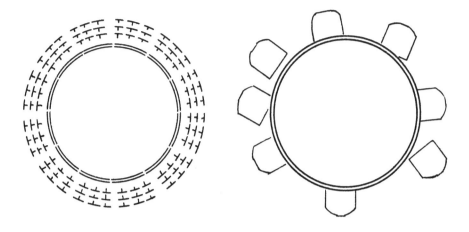

Figure 7.2. Theater in the round.   Figure 7.3. Round table.

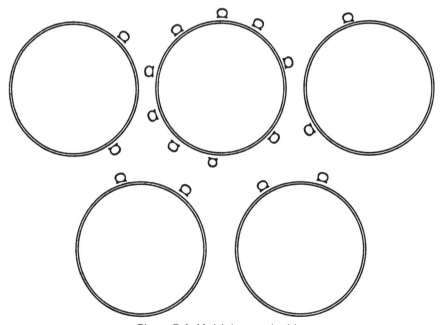

Figure 7.4. Multiple round tables.

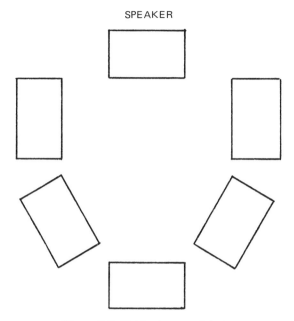

Figure 7.5. Tables in a semicircle.

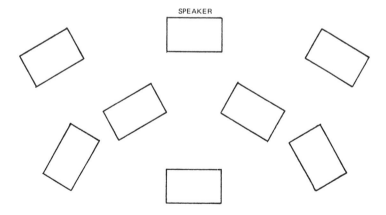

Figure 7.6. Semicircle in multiple rows.

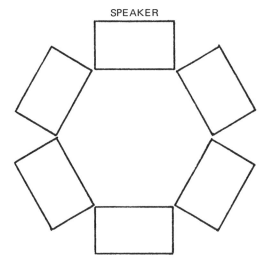

Figure 7.7. Hexagon.

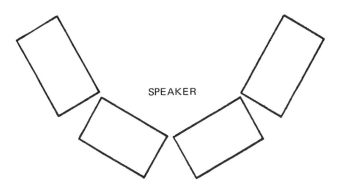

Figure 7.8. Trisected circle.

SPEAKER

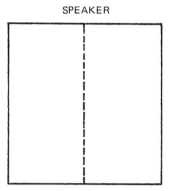

Figure 7.9. Small square.

SPEAKER

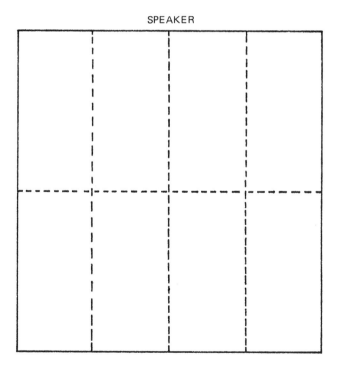

Figure 7.10. Large, solid square.

SPEAKER

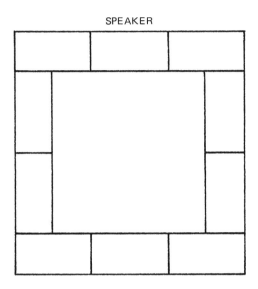

Figure 7.11. Large, open square.

SPEAKER

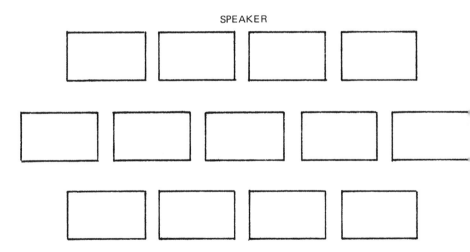

Figure 7.12. Rows of open tables.

SPEAKER

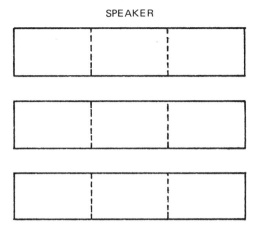

Figure 7.13. Rows of closed tables.

SPEAKER

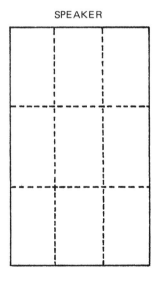

Figure 7.14. Large, solid rectangle.

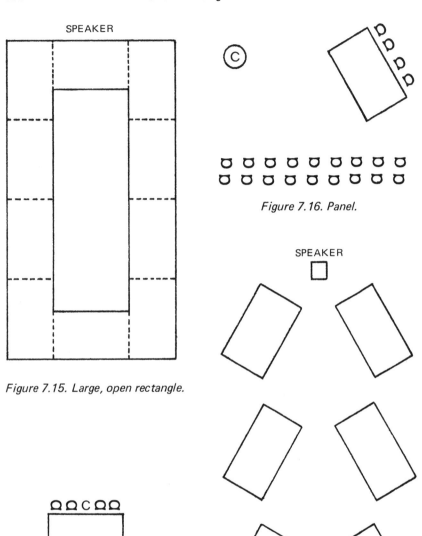

SPEAKER

Figure 7.16. Panel.

Figure 7.15. Large, open rectangle.

Figure 7.17. Panel (C is chairman).   Figure 7.18. Herring-bone (C is chairman).

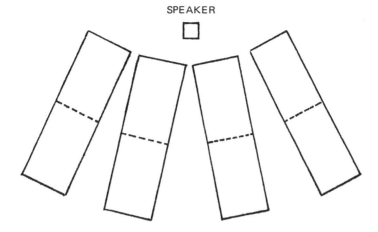

Figure 7.19. Wheel.

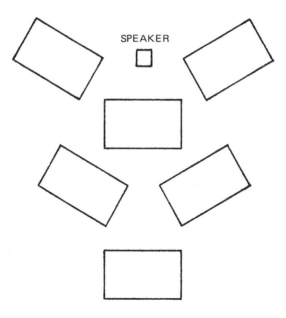

Figure 7.20. Island.

SPEAKER

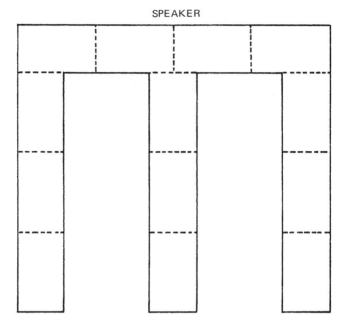

Figure 7.21. E.

SPEAKER

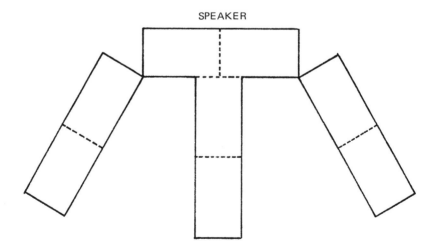

Figure 7.22. Open E.

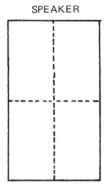

Figure 7.23. Large I.

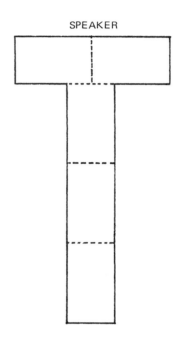

Figure 7.24. T.

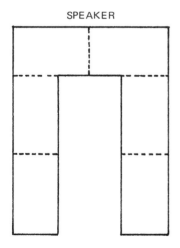

Figure 7.25. U.

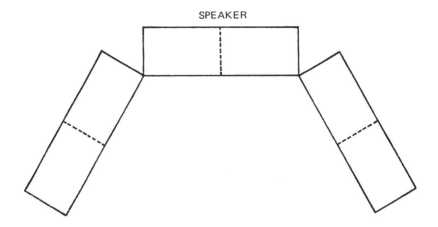

Figure 7.26. Open U.

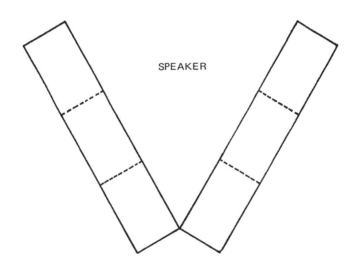

Figure 7.27. V.

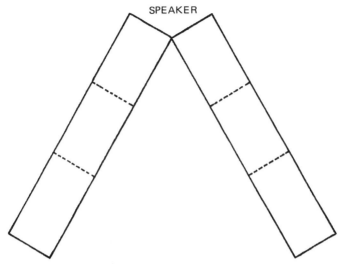

Figure 7.28. Inverted V.

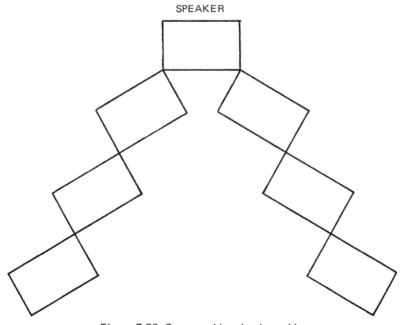

Figure 7.29. Staggered herring-bone V.

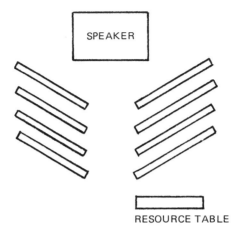

Figure 7.30. Rowed V.

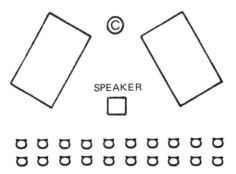

Figure 7.31. Panel V.

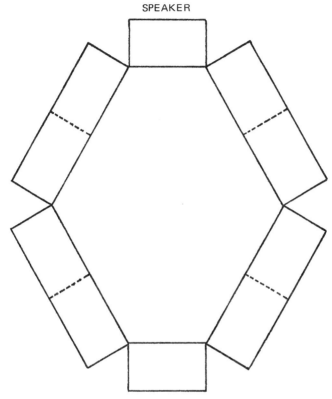

SPEAKER

Figure 7.32. Modified hexagon.

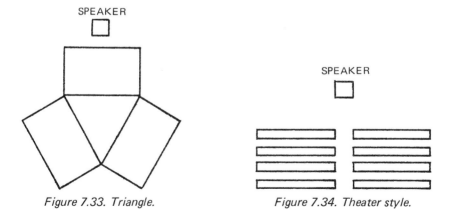

SPEAKER

Figure 7.33. Triangle.

SPEAKER

Figure 7.34. Theater style.

Figure 7.35. Guide for estimating space available.

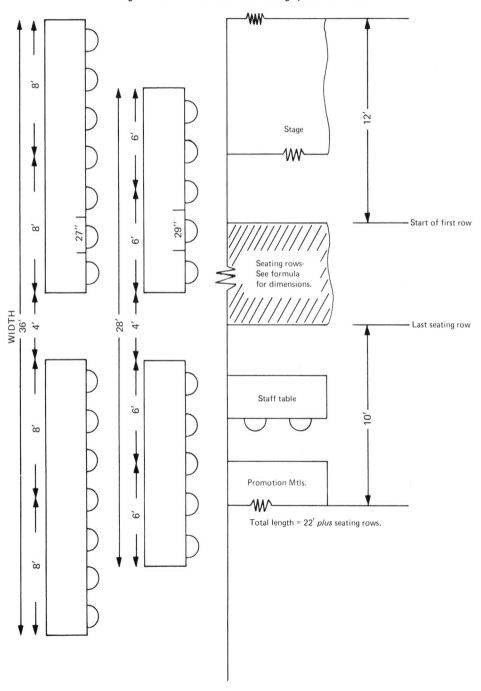

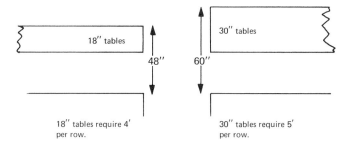

18″ tables require 4′
per row.

30″ tables require 5′
per row.

Formula

1. 6′ x 30″ tables: $\dfrac{\text{No registrants}}{10}$ = No. rows x 5′ per row.

2. 8′ x 30″ tables: $\dfrac{\text{No registrants}}{10}$ = No. rows x 5′ per row.

3. 8′ x 18″ tables: $\dfrac{\text{No registrants}}{14}$ = No. rows x 4′ per row.

Example

54 registrants, 8′ x 18″ tables.

Width: 36′ minimum for 8′ tables

Length: $\dfrac{54}{14}$ = 4 rows x 4′ =   16′

Add: front and rear   22′

Total length   38′

Minimum Room Size = 36′ W x 38′ L

Some of the arrangements are more functional than others. Some are widely employed; others are seldom employed. It must be remembered that the arrangement selected is always a compromise, and trade-off, among size of room, tables and chairs available, number of participants, purpose of the meeting and methodology to be employed.

Determining Room Size

Rooms come in all sizes and shapes. It is not possible to list the space required for all the table and chair constellations that are illustrated. As a rough guide and example, the chart in Figure 7.35 may be found useful. It is reproduced here by permission of The President's Association, Inc., affiliated with the American Management Association, Inc.

Knowledge is not knowledge
until someone else knows
that one knows.

Lucilius (c 125 B.C.)

8
Meeting Planning
Sheet Examples

Frequently the meeting planner reads guidelines on effective planning in books and articles. His reaction often is, "That sounds nice, but does anyone actually use it?" Work sheets used by the Planning and Steering Committee of an actual conference are reproduced in Figures 8.1 through 8.8. The committee was concerned with setting up a three-day conference for 45 in-plant participants at a resort facility located about 100 miles from the plant. The participants included top and middle management personnel. Only two outside persons were involved. Primarily the conference was a fact-finding and confrontation conference. The work sheets were developed by the committee during the several weeks it met preceding the conference. These are not presented as an ideal but rather as a specific example to illustrate many of the concepts and points made in the preceding chapters. Titles and

Figure 8.1. Assignments and things to do.

Done Date	Item	Assigned to*

1. Arrange for bus
   Arrive Gate Z: 10:00 a.m.
   Arrive Hotel: 12:15 p.m.
   Cost: $276.
   Capacity: 54
2. Arrange for private cars
3. Letter to Attendees
   a. Time—place—purpose
   b. Going by bus or car
   c. Hotel reservation arrangements
   d. Dress
   e. Entertainment
   f.   Send agenda
4. Arrange for rooms
5. Arrange meeting rooms
6. Arrange entertainment
7. Arrange for company top management
8. After hours activities
9. Arrange supplies—list of needs;
   how to get it there; repro equipment
10. Equipment needed

*Initials of member of planning and steering committee to which the item was assigned.

Figure 8.2. Equipment and supplies.

Supplied by hotel*	To be supplied by company*	Item	If company provides who is responsible†
		Repro machines—2 portable	
		Electric typewriter	
		Lavalier mike	
		Podium mike	
		File cabinet: 5 drawers, with lock	
		5 by 7 movie screen	
		7 easels	
		2 Vu-graphs	
		Spare bulbs for Vu-graph	
		Adding machine	
		2 portable dictaphones	
		1 projection table	
		1 blackboard—4 by 8	
		Chair and typing table	
		3 phones	
		Lectern	
		3 film (names given)	
		One 16 mm movie projector with spare bulbs	
		Four 4 by 8 foot Homosote Poster Boards with supporting easels	
		Fifty 8½ by 11 pads—for notes	
		100 pencils—sharpened	
		Pencil sharpener	
		Repro paper	
		Ditto masters	
		25 pads for easels	
		Adding machine tapes	
		One 3-hole punch	
		3 packs Vu-graph paper for transparencies	
		1 Scissors	
		7 roll masking tape	
		14 rulers	
		Phone book: local and plant	
		Reference library from Training Office	
		1 box chalk	
		3 erasers	
		24 black magic markers	
		6 red magic markers	
		2 staplers	
		2 boxes staples	
		2 pointers	
		3 erasers	

*A check (✓) should be placed in the appropriate column.

†Initials of person responsible.

Figure 8.3. Problems that arose during planning.

Problem	Assigned for handling*
1. Security check	
2. Entertainment	
3. Time of meetings	
4. After hours liquors and foods	
5. Double-up in rooms	
6. Leave times	
7. People going by car	
8. Emergency phone calls	
9. Check-out procedure at hotel	
10. Procedures for those wanting to attend church Sunday A.M.	
11. Bus schedule back to plant	

*Initials of person to whom problem is assigned.

Figure 8.4. Attendants.

Name	Going by bus	Going by car	Double-up in room?	Room number	Remarks

Figure 8.5. Participant's notebook.

60 plastic with BP Pen. 8½ by 11
To contain:
    List of attendees and their room numbers
    Bio data sheets of resource persons
    Copy of hotel rules
    Agenda
    Copy of Conference objectives
    Tablet

Figure 8.6. Instruction letter to participants include this information.

Data on the bus
First day's activities
    Arrival at hotel at 12:15 p.m.
    Check-in procedures
    Lunch 12:45 in Main Dining Room
    First Session at 2:00 p.m. in Royalty Room

Figure 8.7. Preliminary agenda.

Date

10:00 a.m.	Leave plant for hotel
	a. Baggage checks
	b. Room nos. in advance
	c. Participant's agendas
12:15	Arrive at hotel
12:20	Check in. All rooms assigned by 3:00 p.m.
12:45 p.m.	Lunch. Main dining room buffer or open menu.
2:00	Meeting in Blue Room
	a. Room set up 7 at a table
	b. Secretary outside
	c. 6 small meeting rooms
	d. Floor plan sketched on blackboard
3:45	Coffee break
6:00	Social hour
	Secure private room
	Hors d'oeuvre (hot and cold)
7:00	Dinner. Open menu. Main dining room.
	Displayed sample menu
8:30	Meeting in Blue Room

terminology of the committee have been retained; no attempt has been made to make the items conform to the book's terminology or to translate the committee's work sheets into "ideal planning sheets."

Figure 8.8. Items to include in advance materials sent to participants.

EXHIBIT I

Mail address
Telephone number
Telegram address
Medical provisions
Laundry and dry cleaning
Rooms
Tours
Transportation
Travel reservations
Recreation
Dress
Eating facilities
Map/brochure of facility
Map showing location of facility
Advance reading or preparation

It may be useful to the meeting planner to see additional examples of actual planning sheets used by organizations. Several are shown in Figures 8.9 through 8.13. It should be emphasized

Figure 8.9. Offsite training facility survey (courtesy of North American Rockwell, El Segundo, California). NOTE: Space can be provided at the end of this sheet for more detailed comment by item number and for references if necessary.

Facility Name _____ Address _____

Contact _____ Phone No. _____ Room No. _____

Purpose_____ Dates Req. _____ No. Attendees/GP ____ No. Grps ____
      (Conf/Meeting)

Length of Conf/Meeting _____ Seating Arrangements desired _____

Over-all evaluation/comments (additional space reverse side) _____

_____

_____

Evaluator _____ Date _____

A. MEETING ROOM (Give Size) _____

	*X	S	U
1. Seating Capacity			
2. General appearance			
3. Ingress/Egress Adeqcy.			
4. Noise Level			
5. Proximity to dng/sleepg rms.			
6. Heat/Air Cond/Vent Cntls			
7. Lighting/Lighting Cntls			
8. Tables/Chairs (Comfort)			
9. Elec. outlets (location)			
10. Windows/drapes to drkn rm.			
11. Storage Space (Secure?)			
12. Stability of rm. setup			
13. Mobil/Flex. (Rm arrgmt)			
14. Cleanup Service			
15. Avail/extra mtg rms.			
16. Rest rooms location/size			

17. |Cost| _____

B. TRAINING EQUIPMENT PROVIDED _____
                                (YES—NO)

1. Blackboard _____ Screen _____

2. Lectern _____ Easels _____

3. Chalk/Erasers _____ Pointer _____

4. Projectors Avail.

    a. O/head ___ b. Slide _____ c. Movie _____

5. Tape Recorder_____

6. P. A. System (if needed)_____

7. Other_____

C. MEALS (Obtain Menu) (complete items)

1. Menu Variety   _____

2. Special diets   _____

3. Meal schedule/|Cost| (include tax & tip)

    a. Breakfast   _____

    b. Lunch   _____

    c. Dinner   _____

4. Dining Rm. Seating   _____

5. Minimum Meal Guarantee_____

6. Days advance Notice (mls)_____

7. Other _____

D. SLEEPING ACCOMO. (if applic.)

	X	S	U
1. Prox. to mtg rms/meals			
2. Bed comfort			
3. Cleanliness			
4. Noise insulation			
5. Closet Space			
6. Desk/Desk Light (Stdy Env)			

7. Bath (private/central)   (_____)

8. Room Rates — Single   (_____)

   inc. tax — Double   (_____)

9. Days advance guarantee   (_____)

10. Other_____

Planning Examples   127

E. OTHER SERVICES   (YES—NO)   F. OTHER SERVICES (Complete)

   1. Parking Avail (Free?)   _____ _____   1. Parking Capacity   _____

   2. Ice water for clrms   _____ _____   2. [Cost]—Coffee, Soft Drinks,

   3. Messages/Measage Board   _____ _____   Rolls service   _____

   4. Phone Calls (incmg/outgng) _____ _____   3. Phone Booths (Location) _____

   5. Bar facilities   _____ _____   4. Nearest Medical Fac. _____

   6. Coffee Shop (a.m./p.m.)   _____ _____   _____

                                          Phone _____

                                 5. Other _____

                                 6. Helipad location _____

*X — Excellent   S — Satisfactory   U — Unsatisfactory

NOTE: Comment more in detail by item number (when appropriate)

_____
_____
_____
_____
_____
_____
_____
_____
_____
_____
_____
_____

Secure References (if deemed advisable)

_____ Phone _____

_____ Phone_____

Figure 8.10. General arrangements (courtesy of the American Heart Association).

Meeting: (Title) _____

Staffed By: _____

	SPEAKERS					DISCUSSION LEADERS			
Name	Invited	Accepted	Briefed	"Paper" Requested	Name	Invited	Accepted	Briefed

	RECORDERS					RESOURCE CONSULTANTS		
Name	Invited	Accepted	Briefed	Name	Invited	Accepted	Briefed

Figure 8.11. Program responsibilities (courtesy of the American Heart Association).

MEETING: (Title) _____ Number of persons _____

_____ DATE: _____ DAY OF WEEK: _____ TIME-From: _____ TO: _____ PLACE: _____

TYPE OF MEETING

( ) Breakfast ( ) Luncheon ( ) Dinner Other: (describe) _____

( ) Lecture ( ) Panel ( ) Discussion _____

EQUIPMENT

	No. of Units		No. of Units		No. of Units	
Lighted Lectern		Lapel Mike		3½ x 4 Slides		
Movie Screen		Blackboard		2 x 2 Slides		
Table Mike		16 MM Sound		Record Player		
Standing Mike		16 MM Silent				

SPEAKERS' TABLE	MENU
No. of Persons: _____	
Seating Arrangement: (from left to right facing audience)	
1_____ 9_____	
2_____ 10_____	
3_____ 11_____	
4_____ 12_____	
5_____ 13_____	
6_____ 14_____	
7_____ 15_____	
8_____ 16_____	

STAFF ASSISTANTS FOR FLOOR DETAILS

(Names)

Equipment and physical arrangements _____

Ushering and Seating _____

Messages & Directions _____

Speakers Table _____

Figure 8.12. Meeting planning worksheet (courtesy of the American Cancer Society, Inc.).

American Cancer Society, Inc._____County Unit_____Division

_____ _____ _____ _____
Name of meeting   Date of meeting   Time of meeting   Place of Meeting

Worksheet completed by _____

                              Assignments   follow-up Date   Remarks
_____
Objectives of meeting
_____
Who shall attend?
_____
What do we want to say?
_____
Program participants
_____
What materials will we use?
_____
Methods of presenting
_____
How will audience participate?
_____
Meeting and/or visual aids
_____
Reporting
_____

Figure 8.13. Meeting check list (courtesy of the American Cancer Society, Inc.). NOTE: An X should be placed in the space provided when the assignment or arrangement has been completed. If the item is not applicable, a dash (−) should be placed in the space.

Before the meeting	Target Date	Date Completed

Speakers or participants
_____Written acceptance
_____Written agreement on honorarium
_____Orientation to A.C.S. program
_____List of any special equipment needed
_____Advance information or material

General meeting arrangements
_____Site of meeting
_____Written confirmation of reservation
_____Written agreement on cost of meeting room(s)
_____Written agreement on cost of meals and menus
_____Decision and agreement on meeting facilities required

Promotion and publicity
_____Biographical data on speakers
_____Photos of same
_____Advance copies of speeches or papers
_____Announcement of meeting
_____Contacts with reporters
_____Preparation of posters or flyers
_____Distribution of same
_____Advance mailings
_____Phone followup
_____Preparation of printed program
_____Distribution of same
_____Secure and instruct photographer

Meeting facilities and room arrangements
_____Seating arrangements
_____Speakers' table arrangements. Check on—
_____Location of electrical outlets
_____Location of P.A. controls
_____Where special equipment will be placed
_____Arrangements for press
_____Facilities for social activities

(Figure 8.13 continued on following page)

132 **Small Meeting Planner**

(Figure 8.13 continued)

General
_____Prepare registration cards
_____Prepare badges or name tags
_____Prepare lists of complimentary and prepaid
     reservations
_____Prepare lists of materials, supplies and
     equipment to be taken to the meeting

Time of meeting
_____Complete registration setup
_____Set up identifying sign or poster
_____Final check on arrangements and facilities
_____Final check on special equipment
_____Place cards at head table
_____Set up exhibits or displays
_____Distribute and collect evaluation forms

After the meeting

_____Tips to hotel staff
_____Return borrowed or rented equipment
_____Followup news story
_____Thank you letters
_____Prepare and distribute minutes or proceedings
_____Pay bills
_____Summarize evaluation forms
_____Report to Board of Directors

that these are not displayed as being perfect examples. Rather, they are used to illustrate how many of the concepts discussed look when they are translated into planning sheets and check lists by organizations.

A myriad of check lists have been constructed. None can be generic enough to serve as a specific guide to a specific meeting planner or to meet the needs of a specific organization. The meeting planner is advised to construct his own to meet his own meeting needs.

Knowledge
    which is acquired under compulsion
obtains no hold on the mind.

Plato, The Republic

9
Group Movement
Discussion Techniques

Some meeting planners have very serious meeting purposes and prefer to handle their meetings "straight" and formally. Other meeting planners also have serious meeting purposes but prefer to inject a note of levity or informality into their mechanics. This chapter contains a number of suggestions and techniques that may be useful to both types of meeting planners. They are not included because all of them are believed to be "recommendable" but because the needs of different meeting planners are so varied.

Manipulating People's Movements

The techniques listed in Figure 9.1 have been used to direct, contain or expedite the movement of participants.

Figure 9.1. Techniques to direct, contain or expedite the movement of participants.

1. Ushers can be employed to direct where people sit.
2. Name tents should be placed on tables to indicate seating arrangements.
3. If separate tables are used, the table number is placed on the table, and participant's name tags contain the number of the table at which they are to sit.
4. Back seats should be roped off.
5. Only the front seats should be set up; other chairs should be brought in as they are needed.
6. Seat tickets should be used; the number on the seat corresponds with the number on the participant's registration card.
7. Badges, colors or symbols to match badge, color or symbol of the table or row in which the participant is to sit can be used.
8. Door prizes can be awarded—more prizes for people sitting toward the front.
9. A few "name" people can be seated up front; participants like to sit by them.

Dividing the Group

Obviously, it is no problem to numerically divide a large group into several small groups. However, the composition of the small group may be critical to the effective accomplishment of the group's task. In this instance the meeting planner will devote a great deal of time to the small group composition. In other instances the composition of the small groups will be immaterial to the task accomplishment, and the meeting planner will simply want easy or novel ways to accomplish the groupings. Where the groupings can be critical to the task attainment, the kinds of considerations listed in Figure 9.2 will be useful.

Figure 9.2. Considerations in dividing large groups into small groups.

1. Generally speaking, small groups should contain five to seven participants. Beyond seven members the group loses intimacy, and the size encourages sub-groupings.
2. The feeling of individual responsibility for the success of the task normally decreases as the size of the group increases.
3. Heterogeneity in groups normally increases creativity.
4. "Group think" will almost always outperform "individual think."
5. Periodic change in physical arrangements enhances the advantages of heterogeneous group composition.
6. The use of groups is not a magical tool—putting five ignorant people together usually only produces compounded ignorance.
7. If the group will meet over a time span of several meetings, one or two persons who have good group maintenance skills, should be added to participants with good task skills.
8. The ideal size group is the one that contains the minimum number of task and maintenance skills necessary to accomplish the group task. To exceed this number is to duplicate skills and abilities.
9. As can be seen, the meeting planner must analyze what is the purpose of the small groupings. Once this is done, he can answer the first simple question, "Is the composition of the group at all important?" If it is not, he can proceed to a simple grouping technique. If it is critical, he will then need carefully to analyze the task, the skills and knowledge needed by the participant "mix" to work on the task, to set up criteria for group composition and then to apply these crite-

(Figure 9.2 continued on following page)

(Figure 9.2 continued)

ria to the participants. Usually such a process will answer the questions so often asked about group compositions:

a. Should a big state be placed with a small state?
b. Should a powerful personality be seated with a shy personality?
c. Should well-developed program states be put with poorly developed program states?
d. Should an attempt be made to mix geographic locations, sexes, minority groups, etc.?

Where the composition of the small group is not critical, techniques listed in Figure 9.3 have been used to compose the groups.

Figure 9.3. Novel techniques for dividing large groups into small groups.

1. Give six or seven participants a card on which is printed the name of a song. They go around humming that song until they find all the rest of the members of their group.
2. Groupings can be accomplished by
    a. Eye color
    b. Predominant color of suits or dresses
    c. Color of shoes
    d. Types of shoe heels
3. When distributing programs or registration cards, small pictures of animals flowers or other designs can be used to show who are the members of one group. One animal, flower or design can be circled to appoint the chairman.
4. Chairs can simply be arranged in clusters of the desired number in a group. When all chairs are filled, that group is complete. No chairs can be moved from the cluster.

5. A cluster of chairs can be set up for each group. On the floor, in the center of the cluster, a number can be put on the floor in chalk. Participants have a number that refers to the chair cluster to which they are assigned. One chair position has a small star or other mark. This, it is announced after the clusters are formed, designates the chairman.
6. The number of groups that is desired can be decided, and participants can be counted off by that series of numbers. Then the location where all "ones" will meet, where all "two's" will meet, etc., is announced.
7. People in alternate rows can turn and face the row still facing toward the front. Now, from the side or center, participants count off by threes. Three in each row facing three in the row still looking toward the front now from a group of six.

Sometimes the meeting planner will have a group that will be together for three to five days. He may decide that he would like to have the participants be members of a different small group each day. Further, he would like for each day's small group to be an entirely new grouping—with no duplication of members from other past groupings. Trying to figure out such a matrix is often time-consuming. Matrices in Figures 9.4 through 9.8 will indicate how this can be done for groups of different sizes.

A B C	A B C	A B C	A B C
1 2 3	1 2 3	1 2 3	1 4 7
4 5 6	5 6 4	6 4 5	2 5 8
7 8 9	9 7 8	8 9 7	3 6 9

Figure 9.4. Matrices for dividing nine participants into three groups.

A	B	C	D	E
1	2	3	4	5
6	7	8	9	10
11	12	13	14	15
16	17	18	19	20
21	22	23	24	25

A	B	C	D	E
1	2	3	4	5
7	8	9	10	6
13	14	15	11	12
19	20	16	17	18
25	21	22	23	24

A	B	C	D	E
1	2	3	4	5
9	10	6	7	8
12	13	14	15	11
20	16	17	18	19
23	24	25	21	22

A	B	C	D	E
1	2	3	4	5
10	6	7	8	9
14	15	11	12	13
18	19	20	16	17
22	23	24	25	21

A	B	C	D	E
1	2	3	4	5
8	9	10	6	7
15	11	12	13	14
17	18	19	20	16
24	25	21	22	23

A	B	C	D	E
1	6	11	16	21
2	7	12	17	22
3	8	13	18	23
4	9	14	19	24
5	10	15	20	25

Figure 9.5. Matrices for dividing 25 participants into five groups.

A	B	C	D	E	F	G	H
2	11	40	38	28	9	36	31
16	15	7	1	24	27	23	20
4	10	18	21	34	26	12	19
5	17	14	35	37	22	41	30
8	3	32	33	25	42	6	29
						39	13

A	B	C	D	E	F	G	H
25	8	39	19	31	23	42	24
12	2	41	37	27	15	13	38
35	4	26	6	20	18	40	10
1	9	21	22	5	32	33	11
17	30	29	36	7	34	3	16
						28	14

A	B	C	D	E	F	G	H
36	25	35	14	40	6	1	27
31	29	34	26	10	24	17	4
7	42	22	28	39	20	21	37
15	5	11	3	38	13	32	2
9	23	8	41	12	16	30	18
						19	33

A	B	C	D	E	F	G	H
29	26	36	4	6	38	27	23
42	24	10	15	2	19	37	40
20	12	31	30	11	17	14	25
32	41	28	18	13	35	8	39
22	1	9	5	3	33	34	7
						16	21

A	B	C	D	E	F	G	H
14	39	38	9	1	3	2	6
23	32	20	7	18	21	10	8
27	16	4	34	26	39	24	22
33	36	25	12	42	19	31	17
11	28	13	40	35	30	29	41
						5	15

Figure 9.6. Matrices for dividing 42 participants into eight groups.

A	B	C	D	E	F	G
1	2	3	4	5	6	7
8	9	10	11	12	13	14
15	16	17	18	19	20	21
22	23	24	25	26	27	28
29	30	31	32	33	34	35
36	37	38	39	40	41	42
43	44	45	46	47	48	49

A	B	C	D	E	F	G
1	2	3	4	5	6	7
10	11	12	13	14	8	9
19	20	21	15	16	17	18
28	22	23	24	25	26	27
30	31	32	33	34	35	29
39	40	41	42	36	37	38
48	49	43	44	45	46	47

A	B	C	D	E	F	G
1	2	3	4	5	6	7
12	13	14	8	9	10	11
16	17	18	19	20	21	15
27	28	22	23	24	25	26
31	32	33	34	35	29	30
42	36	37	38	39	40	41
46	47	48	49	43	44	45

A	B	C	D	E	F	G
1	2	3	4	5	6	7
13	14	8	9	10	11	12
18	19	20	21	15	16	17
23	24	25	26	27	28	22
35	29	30	31	32	33	34
40	41	42	36	37	38	39
45	46	47	48	49	43	44

A	B	C	D	E	F	G
1	2	3	4	5	6	7
9	10	11	12	13	14	8
17	18	19	20	21	15	16
25	26	27	28	22	23	24
33	34	35	29	30	31	32
41	42	36	37	38	39	40
49	43	44	45	46	47	48

A	B	C	D	E	F	G
1	2	3	4	5	6	7
11	12	13	14	8	9	10
21	15	16	17	18	19	20
24	25	26	27	28	22	23
34	35	29	30	31	32	33
37	38	39	40	41	42	36
47	48	49	43	44	45	46

A	B	C	D	E	F	G
1	2	3	4	5	6	7
14	8	9	10	11	12	13
20	21	15	16	17	18	19
26	27	28	22	23	24	25
32	33	34	35	29	30	31
38	39	40	41	42	36	37
44	45	46	47	48	49	43

A	B	C	D	E	F	G
1	8	15	22	29	36	43
2	9	16	23	30	37	44
3	10	17	24	31	38	45
4	11	18	25	32	39	46
5	12	19	26	33	40	47
6	13	20	27	34	41	48
7	14	21	28	35	42	49

Figure 9.7. Matrices for dividing 49 participants into seven groups.

A	B	C	D	E	F	G	H	I	J
6	19	55	2	43	11	53	47	12	33
37	52	23	41	1	20	10	44	49	4
15	35	9	51	58	40	13	16	21	32
36	25	27	18	48	9	45	14	59	39
57	8	54	60	26	3	5	24	30	46
7	56	38	28	17	50	22	31	42	34

A	B	C	D	E	F	G	H	I	J
33	2	39	5	60	24	56	18	54	25
26	3	14	38	30	15	51	4	34	42
28	46	8	31	45	49	44	36	53	55
12	6	58	57	20	13	50	17	7	43
19	9	40	48	32	35	27	11	16	10
23	47	22	1	29	52	59	21	41	37

A	B	C	D	E	F	G	H	I	J
32	43	37	25	16	27	36	54	6	28
48	11	29	46	50	9	7	2	1	35
18	24	33	15	8	41	39	26	20	17
42	53	21	58	51	56	47	3	22	13
44	14	19	4	10	59	52	40	55	60
30	49	57	34	38	12	23	5	45	31

A	B	C	D	E	F	G	H	I	J
10	22	60	47	35	31	46	34	40	41
29	1	56	12	33	42	21	45	9	52
38	16	49	32	44	39	20	50	28	24
4	13	6	3	53	54	14	48	37	7
59	51	11	55	2	18	57	15	8	27
58	30	26	17	23	19	43	25	5	36

A	B	C	D	E	F	G	H	I	J
46	41	48	50	13	4	49	8	51	11
31	17	3	6	5	60	19	56	57	14
34	45	36	37	47	44	32	30	25	53
27	59	52	10	28	43	38	29	26	15
2	23	42	35	21	22	16	33	24	12
20	40	1	54	7	58	18	55	39	9

Figure 9.8. Matrices for dividing 60 participants into 10 groups.

Figure 9.9. Effective warm-up techniques.

1. Experienced persons can meet, in advance, with small groups of participants to find out their expectations, needs, problems, where they feel comfortable and uncomfortable, etc. This information is then fed back to the discussion leaders before their meeting with the small groups. Obviously this means the discussion leaders must be very flexible and able to capitalize upon the information provided.
2. The meeting can be opened with a role play which highlights the problems to be discussed.
3. Confrontation episodes, filmed, taped or played with live actors, can be used to let participants experience how well they can handle the confrontation and where they need help.
4. A film highlighting the meeting focus can be shown.
5. Introduction of participants can be used to highlight the meeting purposes.
6. A problem identification inventory can be scheduled as the first event; the participant identified problems must relate to the meeting content.
7. A cocktail party or coffee is an useful technique to help participants "get on board."

Warm-Up Techniques

Often the meeting planner is concerned with getting the total group off to a fast start, to help participants set norms and standards for their work or to develop a "mind set" in all participants before they go into their small groups to work on a task.

Figure 9.10. Small group discussion expediter techniques.

1. Groups should be allowed to examine quickly the problem and to identify pros and cons of the problem, to immediate reactions, etc. These are written down. Lists are exchanged with another group.

2. If the small group discussion revolves around written material or if the discussion leader can find a short, appropriate written piece of material pertinent to the problem, the "read-around" method can be used; each participant reads a paragraph and then, in his own words, explains what it means to him.

3. A variation of the "read-around" method is that of having the discussion leader describe the group task; each participant then is given no more than one minute to react to the task or his understanding of it.

4. The slip technique calls for the group leader to describe the group task; then each person writes his ideas about the task on 3 by 5 cards—one idea per card. These are then collected and exchanged with another group. The cards are "dealt out" to the group members, and the members react to the ideas on the cards—mingling their own ideas as they go along.

5. The group leader describes the group task. In advance he has collected photographs and small objects related to the task and placed each in an envelope. These are then distributed to the participants, and they open their envelope and react to the content as it relates to the group task.

6. People like to pair; after describing the task, people can be allowed to pair for a few minutes to discuss the group task and then to report to the group.

7. Group members, after the task is discussed and understood, can be allowed a few minutes to reflect individually on the problem and then to announce their thinking before going on to group discussion.

8. Members can be permitted to meet at homes (if meeting is local) or in rooms with roommates to discuss the group task before they come to the meeting for discussion in small groups.

Figure 9.11. Total group discussion expediter techniques.

1. An electrical device can be rigged so that, if participants are seated at table groups, the group can press a
   button and have a light at the front of the room flash
   their table number for recognition. A simpler variation is to provide each table with a placard on a pole.
   The placard has the group's table number printed on
   it. When the group wants to be recognized, a member
   of the group raises and jiggles the placard.
2. One discussion group can occupy the center of the
   floor and discuss the issue while other participants sit
   around the group and take notes. Listening participants can send up notes to a member of the discussion group. Another variation is to stop the discussion
   after about 12 minutes and let the discussion group
   members interact with the listening members for
   about five minutes and then resume their discussion.
   The discussion later is opened to the total group.
3. Small flip charts, containing critical points, tables,
   statistics, etc., paralleling the speaker's presentation,
   can be given to each participant. A spiral bound pad
   about 4 by 6 inches is a good size. The participants
   make notes on the pad of things they want to discuss
   with the speaker during the discussion period.
4. Each person writes down one question he would like
   to ask. These are collected for each row, shuffled and
   given to the participant at the end of the row away
   from the center aisle. He deletes one question he
   thinks is least important and passes the remaining
   questions to the next person, and the process is repeated. The question remaining after the last person
   in the row makes his selection is the question that
   row asks the speaker.
5. Two or three discussion periods can take place during
   the presentation—not just at the end of the discussion.

6. Special listening teams can be appointed. For instance, the audience can be divided into thirds and each third given a task during the presentation: i.e., "What does the speaker say with which you strongly disagree?"; "What does the speaker say with which you strongly agree?"

7. A reacting panel which is seated on stage can be appointed; they are to listen to the presentation with this task in mind, "What questions do I think members of the audience will have?"

Most groups experience awkwardness as they begin to work, particularly if the group has not worked together before. There is an underlying fear that discussion will be difficult to get started and that the members will be overly nice to each other. For this reason, often the first idea thrown out is discussed out of all proportion to its merit and importance. The meeting leader wants techniques to avoid this dynamic. Meeting planners should also know that most often groups are never given enough time to handle their task. If possible, the group should have some voice in setting the amount of time they think they need. In discussing techniques, the meeting planner should be aware that they are techniques only. If the group is ready to work on the problem, no technique is required. Lastly, no technique should be so obvious, complex or obtrusive that the group's attention is devoted to serving the technique and the group's task is relegated to secondary consideration. Several techniques are utilized to accomplish these purposes; Figures 9.9 and 9.10 list some of the more effective.

Discussion Expediters in Total Group

Sometimes the meeting planner is concerned with getting questions and answers in the total group, with expediting reporting and getting relevant discussion or getting discussion started in the total group. Techniques listed in Figure 9.11 may be useful.

Very few men are wise by their own counsel:
or learned by their own teaching.
For he that was only taught by himself,
had a fool for his master.

Ben Johson, Explorata

10
Small Group
Leadership Team

One of the most frequently employed methodologies in meetings is group discussion. The groups can vary in size from seven to 25 members. The optimum size, for full discussion, seems to be from seven to 12. Most often a presentation is made to the total meeting population, and the participants then go into small groups to discuss the presentation or to explore some phase of it. At other times the participants go directly into small groups for an assigned task without a presentation. In most instances, some kind of a report to the total group is expected.

Several tasks face the group leader, who may be appointed in advance or may be selected by the group. He is faced with helping the group to work on its task; he may be expected to have some expertise in the task content area; he is expected to be able to diagnose the processes within the group; and he is expected to be cognizant of the maintenance needs of the group. Often this is too much to expect.

For this reason, it has become customary to divide these roles among other participants. The most common division of work is between the discussion leader and the recorder. Sometimes the discussion leader will report the group's findings to the total group; at other times the recorder will report the group's finding. For larger groups other resource leadership functions are given to participants. This chapter will discuss the functions of the most frequently designated leadership team members. These are the discussion leader, recorder, reporter, process observer and blackboard secretary.

Selecting the leadership team is critical. Usually the meeting planners know many nominees or know where in the organization to find them. One excellent lead can be to look at people who in the past have been nominated for various offices. Another technique is to look at people who are currently holding offices in organizations outside the organization sponsoring the meeting. Still another lead is to consider those persons whose names are mentioned frequently by a group. One word of caution is indicated here: often informal leaders do not make effective leaders of discussion groups.

Good criteria for leadership team selection do not exist. Much, of course, depends upon the kind of group and the task it is given to solve. Technical expertise may be mandatory in the leaders. More often, the major criteria will be leaders who know and understand group processes and discussion techniques, who have good conceptual ability and who do not have status and ego needs that will get in their way of letting the group work effectively.

If a number of small groups are to be used, most meeting planners have found it highly desirable to train the leadership teams. If they are already skilled in their functions, then they should be oriented to this particular meeting and its objectives. The main objectives of a meeting can be defeated if the small group leadership teams do not fully comprehend the meeting objectives and the role the small meeting tasks play in contributing to these objectives. Sometimes the briefing occurs the evening before the meeting; at other times it occurs in the morning before the first main meeting session. Generally the early morning breakfast orientation sessions are not desirable. Too often the maintenance needs of the leadership teams delays the orientation; those involved in orienting the teams have other concerns pressing on them; and there is not sufficient time for a thoughtful planning session.

One overall useful model is to have an orientation meeting the night before. It may or may not be held in connection with dinner and cocktails. If cocktails are served, they should be kept at a minimum. Group members are briefed on the overall purpose of the meeting. They are familiarized with the leadership teams and meet the members of their own team. Functional leaders then meet for a while with a resource person for particular briefing— that is, all discussion leaders meet together; all reporters meet together; and so on. At this briefing, individual functional aids are distributed, such as handouts, check lists, evaluation forms and statement of the task. Following these functional briefing meetings, the teams meet together to discuss further plans for their small groups.

One word of caution must be raised. Meeting planners sometimes fall into the trap of calling such orientation meeting "training in discussion methods" or "leadership training." An adequate discussion leader cannot be trained within a short span of time. Little is done to remedy this illusion if persistence in calling a half-hour meeting a training session for leaders is continued. The meeting planner must select already competent discussion and group leaders. These sessions are nothing but orientation sessions for this particular meeting. This function is critical, a leader is not going to be developed from raw material in 30 minutes.

During the planning session, those responsible for orientation should take special pains to see that the following are well understood by all members of the leadership team:

1. The overall meeting purposes and objectives.
2. The specific objectives and tasks of the small groups and how this relates to the main meeting purposes.
3. The criteria used for placing participants in the small groups.

4. Any handouts or reference materials for either participants or leadership team and where and how these will be made available to the team.

5. Meeting room assignments and instructions for locating the room (it is best to have the leadership team inspect the room before the group meets).

6. The system of reporting to be used which includes the reports to the larger group and any special plans for reports to be made to the meeting planner for later reproduction and distribution.

7. If coffee or other breaks are involved, specific information on time and place.

The duties of each member of the leadership team will vary with the needs of the group, the objectives of the meeting and the individual preferences of the meeting planners. Many instructions and techniques have been developed for the various functional team members. It has been the experience of most meeting planners that it is best not to overwhelm the team members with reams of instructions, techniques, guides, etc. Useful reminders to cover with the discussion leader are given in Figure 10.1.

Figure 10.1. Duties of the discussion leader.

A. Advance preparation
  1. If the discussion leader is selected in advance of the meeting, he should involve members of his group through letters, questionnaires, interviews and suggestions.
  2. Resources and aids for the group should be selected; this could be film, film strips, brief articles or resource documents, recordings, a resource person, etc.
  3. He must understand fully the objectives of the overall meeting and the specific objectives of the small group meetings. What is to be the specific outcome of his group if its work is successful?

(Figure 10.1 continued on following page)

4. He should organize his own ideas; he is one of the group's resources. What is his position on the task content? What are some relevant questions? How will he begin?

B. Physical arrangements

If possible, he should visit the group meeting room in advance to get a "feel" of it and know how to give directions to others on how to reach it. He may want to place a sign outside the room. As appropriate, he should check off his needs using the following list:

1. Is it large enough to accomodate all participants?
2. Are tables available so all can have a space? Round, square or rectangular are about equally good.
3. Are there enough chairs?
4. Lighting.
5. Ventilation.
6. Temperature controls.
7. Blackboard, eraser, chalk.
8. Chart pad and magic markers.
9. Water and glasses.
10. Ashtrays.
11. Audio-visual equipment: in readiness with a trained operator.
12. Extension cord.
13. Electric outlets.
14. Handouts or other materials to be distributed. Where do you get them?
15. Name tents.
16. Pencils and paper.
17. Masking tape.
18. Provision for outer wraps.
19. Restroom facilities.
20. If coffee is to be served, what are the times and arrangements?

C. Leading the group

1. The discussion leader should introduce himself and the other group leadership team members and briefly explain their roles.

2. If he knows it, he should explain the criteria used in composing the groups.

3. The objective of the total meeting should be explained as well as the relationship of the group task to the overall objective. He must make certain that everyone understands the task.

4. Introductions may or may not be needed. The time allowed should be appropriate to the overall time available and how much the leader senses the need for introductions and for members to know the kinds of resources they have in the group.

5. The discussion leader should never apologize in his opening remarks on his inadequacy or that "a million others could do as well." He must not confuse humility with servility. His mental attitude of self-sufficiency and assuredness can be most contagious.

6. He should try to set an example of confrontation, search and coping. Depending upon the group task, he should get pertinent questions and data out first and try to get off to an animated start, avoiding the *anybody-got-a-question?* approach.

7. The discussion must be kept on the track. The leader must be particularly alert to interesting but nonrelevant trends and inputs– including his own.

8. If some aspect is being neglected, it must be pointed out. If the group does not pick it up, at least the leader has given them the chance.

9. When conclusions, agreement or major points have concensus, they should be tested with the group. If the group agrees, the recorder must get the point down for reporting purposes.

10. The leader should do what he can to involve all members of the group. The key here is opportunity to participate; noncontributing members should not be forced or embarrassed to get involved against their will. Full participation does not mean equal participation.

(Figure 10.1 continued on following page)

(Figure 10.1 continued below and on following page)

11. The leader must remember he is normally not "selling an idea, solution or approach." He is there to release the expertise of the group and to ascertain their best findings.

12. He should encourage leveling and openness. He should not let the group avoid conflict unless it will adversely affect the group's operation; rather he should help the group resolve conflict or at least understand the key issues in the conflict.

13. The leader may find it useful to help the group form a tentative agenda and to think through a timetable for the use of the time alloted to it.

14. If other leadership members are used, they must be considered for their contributions in making the meeting as effective as possible.

15. The leader must know his own biases and be prepared to handle contributions constructively that may violate them.

16. He must be on the alert for decision making before the problem is understood or all data has been surfaced.

17. The meeting should be kept informal, but it should not degenerate into license.

18. Group discussions and concensus should be encouraged rather than letting the groups use the leader as the sanctioning agent.

19. The leader should watch for two or more ideas being worked on simultaneously and help the group to recognize the confusion, to identify the different points and to work on them one at a time.

20. He should be alert for repetition of ideas and call attention to what he sees and ask for group confirmation. If they agree, they should be encouraged to dig deeper.

21. He should attempt to help the group differentiate opinions from facts. Opinions can be very valid, but they need to be identified.
22. Overall time must be watched. Often too much time is spent on the first idea thrown out. The group should be encouraged to pace itself— time for concensus and agreement on the report to be made to the main group must be scheduled.
23. The leader should help the group periodically to summarize where it is and has yet to go.
24. He should establish the value that any person making a contribution is doing so very sincerely in the light of his best knowledge and understanding.
25. He should make use of the blackboard or chart pad to note agenda, main points, concensus items, etc.
26. Finally, he must end the discussion on time.

D. After the group meeting
1. A few moments should be spent with the recorder to be sure of the points to be reported and the manner in which the report will be made.
2. If questions were unanswered or dimensions presented themselves which may not be known by the meeting planners, these should be submitted to them.
3. If reports, other than reports to the total group, are to be made, the leader should follow up to be sure who is to submit the report and that it is submitted.

In briefing different members of the leadership team, it is often found desirable to give them a short handout setting forth their main duties, things to watch and advance preparation. The materials for other members of the leadership team (Figures 10.2 through 10.6) were designed so that they could be duplicated and given to them. Some of the items included have already been covered in more detail earlier in the book but are repeated here for the reason just mentioned.

Recorder

The recorder normally is responsible for recording, in writing, a bold summary of the group's discussion. This will include major agreements, disagreements and recommendations. This may be kept on notepaper or placed on chart pad paper for presentation to the total group. Sometimes the report is put on a chart pad for the total group report and submitted later to a conference official in notepaper form for record purposes, duplication or study and consolidation reasons. The recorder may be asked to make the group's report to the main group, or this may be done by either the reporter, if one is appointed, or the group discussion leader. Sometimes the functions of the recorder, reporter and group discussion leader are all given to the discussion leader. At other times the functions of the recorder and reporter are combined in the reporter. These functions are listed in Figure 10.2.

Figure 10.2. Functions of the recorder.

1. The recorder should plan with the group discussion leader the way they will work. The group leader should indicate to the recorder when he thinks items should be made a matter of record.
2. If a report is to be submitted to a meeting planner, the recorder must make sure to indicate on his report:
   a. Date and time the group met.
   b. Group number or other designator.
   c. Meeting room.
   d. Name of discussion leader.
   e. His name as recorder.
   f. Task given to the group.
   g. If possible, he should retain a carbon copy of the report for his records.
   h. Date and time he submitted the report.
3. If a special recording or reporting format is to be used, he must make sure he understands it.

4. He must indicate the task of the group.
5. He must note the main points, facts and issues that emerge in the discussion. The recorder should not attempt to record all points made and the individual contributions of members or try to keep a running commentary of the discussion. What he is after are the critical, main discussion points, issues, decisions, recommendations and resolutions.
6. He should note any problems left unresolved.
7. All agreements reached should be noted.
8. The recorder should also note all major disagreements.
9. All recommendations should be recorded.
10. If there is disagreement on how something should be worded, the order of items or whether items should be included, the group and the discussion leader should make the decision. This may be difficult when the recorder has strong feelings about the decision, but his first obligation is his duties as a recorder. One of the points that should be made clear to the discussion leader and the group is whether the recorder is to function solely as a recorder or as a participant/recorder.
11. The recorder must be prepared to summarize periodically the items he has noted as significant to have reported out by the group.
12. If he is not sure whether an item is important to record, he should ask the discussion leader or the group.
13. If he does not understand conclusions, recommendations or main points, he must not hesitate to ask the group to clarify.
14. He must also be prepared, toward the end of the group meeting, to summarize for the group the items to be reported. The group may wish to change or delete items.

(Figure 10.2 continued on following page)

(Figure 10.2 continued)

15. As he records, he should look for a pattern and outline that will make his summary understandable and cohesive. Sometimes the group's output lends itself to headings such as "Problems," "Decisions," "Recommendations," "Problems Not Discussed," "Disagreements" and "Unusual Idea." He should organize his report as the discussion moves along.
16. If his summary is kept on the chart pad, as sheets are filled they should be removed from the pad and hung with masking tape on a suitable surface so that all sheets can be seen by the participants at all times.

Reporter

It is customary for either the discussion leader or the recorder to make the group's report to the main group. Sometimes a separate person is appointed to perform this function. Regardless who performs this duty, the suggestions in Figure 10.3 will help to make the report effective.

Figure 10.3. Guidelines for the reporter.

1. In advance, the reporter should check with the discussion leader on whether the report should be made verbally, and whether copies of his report should be duplicated for distribution to all members of the main group or placed on chart pad paper to be hung before the total group as he discusses the points. The latter is currently the most widely used technique.
2. He should make sure his points are organized well, print in letters large enough for all to see and have masking tape available to hang the sheets. Some chart pads will permit multiple sheets to be suspended as a "bundle" and the pages turned as the report progresses.

3. The reporter is not expected to make a speech. Usually three to five minutes are sufficient to make the report.

4. He must not attempt to reconstruct the meeting but report quickly on the main points discussed, the issues identified, the decisions, recommendations or resolutions reached, unresolved issues and minority reports.

5. The resource person controlling the reporting session will indicate if the reporter should "stand by" for questions. The normal procedure is to permit participants to ask clarification questions only. The general discussion takes place after all reports are made. The reporter's role is to be sure the points his group made are understood—he is not to defend them at this time.

6. If the chart pad or similar reporting aid is used, it can be used effectively to help summarize the report from the group. Even though it is written, it is good to read the points and to add a bit of clarification since most points will be recorded sketchily on the chart pad. Avoid pointing to the chart pad and saying, "There it is—it speaks for itself." Seldom will the notes on the chart pad speak for themselves.

Observer

A group always works at two levels—task and maintenance. A leader attempts to analyze how effectively the group is functioning at both levels. Often this is very difficult to do, and the leader will use a member of the leadership team to act as observer. The observer usually is not an active participant since it is difficult to take part in the discussion and at the same time observe the processes within the group. The observer constantly diagnoses the group and the processes that are occurring. Is too much time being taken on a small point? Are proper task skills being employed? Is the group neglecting its own maintenance? What skills or insights would be useful to the group at a given time? The suggestions in Figure 10.4 will be useful.

Figure 10.4. Duties of the observer.

1. The observer should consult with the discussion leader and other members of the leadership team in advance, define his role and determine if the leader will ask him for suggestions during the meeting or whether he is free to make suggestions at any time he thinks they would be useful.
2. He should make sure the leader identifies him to the group and explains his role.
3. Things that seem to help or hinder the group in its work should be noted.
4. The observer must make notes, but he should not be conspicuous by frantic scribbling.
5. When he reports to the group, he should not make a speech or lecture. His role is to reflect processes the group may not see because of the animated discussion.
6. Generally it is best for the observer not to tell the group what he thinks they should do; instead, he should report what he observes is hindering the group and let them decide the steps to be taken.
7. He should take special pains not to be offensive to anyone.
8. One common technique, particularly if the group is to meet over a period of several meetings, is to spend the last five to 10 minutes of the session in helping the group to look at how well they worked as a group. The leader and the observer may decide this is the point at which the observer will make his contribution and lead the group as it examines its processes.

9. Sometimes special reaction or diagnostic sheets are used at the end of the session to collect data on how the meeting went and how the functioning of the members could be improved. If this is done, the observer should take responsiblity for explaining the sheets, collecting the data and tabulating the results for the group.
10. What should the observer report on? Such things as:
    a. Was the group task clear to all members?
    b. Was the problem well defined?
    c. Did the group elicit good facts? Did they use them?
    d. Did conflict arise? If so, how well was it handled?
    e. Did all feel free to participate?
    f. Did a few monopolize the discussion?
    g. Was the leader responsive to the group's needs?
    h. Was too much time spent on insignificant items?
    i. Did the group engage in flight behavior?
    j. Was there a turning point? If so, what precipitated it?
    k. Did the group use its time effectively?
    l. Were there any signs of "hidden agendas"?

Resource Person

Sometimes a resource person is made part of the leadership team. This tends to occur when the task is complex or the group may not have, in its membership, some pertinent data it will require to make intelligent decisions and recommendations. The resource person is often an "outsider"—even if with the organization, he is outside the group. He is not a full-fledged member of the group. His knowledge, skills and experiences are being made available to the group if it needs them. This is a difficult role to play. Too often the resource person will be seen as an expert, and the group will unduly turn to him for advice, knowledge, and procedures and let him monopolize the total time. The suggestions in Figure 10.5 will assist the resource person in being effective.

Figure 10.5. Suggestions to make the resource person more effective.

1. The resource person should meet with the discussion leader and the other members of the leadership team in advance and discuss his mutual roles and how he will operate.
2. He will not make speeches.
3. He must be careful not to take the leadership away from the discussion leader.
4. When asked for help, he should provide data as needed and avoid giving his advice unless it is pertinent. He should help the discussion leader by "throwing" the discussions and questions back to the group. If he could accomplish the task given to the group, it would have been senseless to appoint a group.
5. He should help the group clarify the problem.
6. He should also help the group test the validity of its process and thinking. Often this can be done by asking a pertinent question at the right time.
7. He must remember that his primary role is to provide facts that may not be available to the group. A good guide is, "Will my participation at this point really help the group in its deliberations or will it primarily serve my ego and status needs?"
8. If the resource person has taken up the major portion of time alloted to the group for its task, the odds are pretty heavy that he has not performed his role well.

Blackboard/Chart Pad Secretary

Occasionally a group will want to have the recorder seated while taking notes for later use by the meeting planners. The discussion leader may desire to place the agenda developed by the group, major issues identified and decisions and recommendations on a blackboard or chart pad. In this instance a blackboard/chart pad secretary may be used for this function. Normally he does not make the group's report. When the meeting is concluded, his function has been served. The suggestions given for the recorder (Figure 10.2) are useful for him to review since they include most of the useful guides. In addition, the techniques and reminders in Figure 10.6 will be helpful.

Figure 10.6. Techniques and reminders for the blackboard/chart pad secretary.

1. The blackboard/chart pad secretary should meet in advance with the discussion leader and other members of the leadership team to outline his role.
2. The leader should identify the secretary to the group and make clear his role.
3. The secretary will provide a visual record of agreements reached and the flow of the group's work.
4. He will list the tentative agenda developed by the group, the major items identified and discussed, the decisions and actions, the recommendations and resolutions reached, and he will indicate minority positions and questions or issues left unresolved.
5. The group and discussion leader will help him decide when items are to be recorded.
6. If a chart pad is used, he must make sure he has masking tape to hang the sheets as they are filled.
7. He must write large enough for all to see. Printing is recommended.

(Figure 10.6 continued on following page)

(Figure 10.6 continued)

8. He will be required to write rapidly but legibly and to condense long items but to retain understanding.

9. He must be as unobtrusive as possible. He must not censor or quarrel with items—the group and discussion leader are the determiners of what should be recorded.

10. He should not stand, as he writes, so as to hide the writing surface.

11. Since the secretary has a visible position, he should be careful not to be seen as vying with the discussion leader. During long periods of discussion, it is best for the secretary to have a chair near by and to sit down so the leader is visibly the leader.

Random Selection of Leadership Team Members

Most tasks selected for a group to work on are important to the meeting planners and to the group members. For this reason, much thought, planning and preparation should be given to the selection of the leadership team members. However, occasionally a task is such that the group can select any member to provide the functions needed. In these instances, selection of leaders can quickly and humorously be accomplished by light-hearted selection techniques. The following will indicate ways in which this can be accomplished. (Never use an item that could be embarrassing.)

1. Rotate the leadership alphabetically
2. One with wildest tie
3. The most handsome
4. The most mod dress
5. One with most/least hair
6. Shortest
7. Tallest
8. Oldest

9. Least tenure on present job
10. Most tenure on present job
11. One with predominance of a given color
12. Who has traveled longest way to meeting
13. Who has traveled shortest way to meeting
14. One whose birthday is nearest the day's date
15. Put cards under seat pads, on in light chalk on floor, to indicate which chair is what leadership position
16. Latecomer

What you don't know,
somebody else is getting paid for knowing.

Anonymous

11
Responsibility of Participants

Thus far, as is true of most books dealing with successful meetings, the meeting planner has been the focus of attention. Usually, the entire burden of running a successful meeting is placed squarely upon the shoulders of those who plan the meetings.

But what of the reverse side of this coin? Does not the participant share some of the responsibility? He does. Until recent years, in the communication between a speaker and a listener, most of the responsibility was placed upon the speaker. For example, in debating or interviewing, if the debate or interview was not won, it was assumed the speaker was doing something faulty. Today, in these settings, attention is focused upon such exchanges as a totality with both the speaker and listener bearing equal responsibility for the success of the dialogue.

Increasingly most professionals and, to a lesser degree, all other members of organizations will have to consider education and training a lifetime job. No longer can education be confined to the first three decades of one's life. Much evidence has also accumulated that indicates the learner learns most when is is actively involved in the learning process. He must take the initiative to determine what he needs to know and actively pursue his learning goals. No longer can he sit passively and expect the resource persons to anticipate his every learning need and then blame the resource person if his needs are not met. He has a responsibility to help the resource person meet his needs. The model most often followed today in meetings is that "attaining the meeting objectives is a joint responsibility of the meeting planner and the meeting attender."

The meeting attender is often paid to attend the meeting. He needs to reflect upon, "Why was my organization willing to pay my salary, my travel and maintenance and the meeting fees?" Attendance at a meeting involves the investment of a great deal of money. The following are some of the kinds of questions that participants need to ask:

1. "Why is my organization sending me to this meeting?"
2. "In the final analysis, I am the one who has the most to gain. The organization wants a job done well, but whether it is me or some other employee is not highly important to the organization. This is a privilege for me."
3. "The planners tried to put together a good meeting. Did I really help them with my suggestions as to what I needed and wanted?"

Of course the meeting planners have the responsibility of expediting this process. Did they attempt to involve the participants in planning the meeting? Did they ask the participants for agenda suggestions? Did they try to assess the needs of the participants?

Did they send out the agenda in advance? Did they assign advanced reading assignments if these were appropriate? If participants were to serve as resource persons (observers, discussion leaders, recorders), were they notified in advance, and did they receive helpful briefings?

Figure 11.1. Responsibilities of participants.

1. First, the participant should determine whether or not this is the proper meeting for him to attend—not all meetings are for all people. He should check the brochures, other people who have attended or write for more information and, especially for the agenda.
2. He should separate clearly whether he is attending because the meeting will be useful to him or his organization or whether he is unduly influenced by combining the meeting with a vacation or other personal goals. These can be valid; they can also result in neither goal being accomplished. It is unfair to meeting planners to be confronted with a group of participants whose personal agendas are uppermost in their minds.
3. He should ask, if the organization is paying his way, "Would I attend if I were paying my own way?" "If I were bearing the cost of sending me to this meeting, knowing what I know why I am attending and my mind set, would I send me?" The organization has a right to expect it will get its money worth from his attendance. One helpful technique for the participant is to remember he is on salary while attending the meeting; he should give the organization a full days meeting work for its pay.

4. If advance reading is assigned, or if the participant is asked to discuss the meeting task with others before coming, he must discharge these responsibilities. Normally the meeting planners do not make such requests without much thought and without having a good reason in mind.

5. He must arrive on time; latecomers disrupt the others, and it is discourteous to cause other people to wait while the late arrivals are brought up to date. Seldom is one's individual time worth the cumulative time of the other participants.

6. Participants should stay sober and avoid late card parties, bull sessions and night life. It is patently unfair to the meeting planners, resource persons and other participants to have hung-over members in their midst. The jokes such a participant will hear aimed in his direction are not altogether humorous—if he listens, he will hear the bite of the other participants' true feelings. The kindest thing he can do is to stay home or at least to stay in his room.

7. The participant must understand the purposes of the meeting and ask, "What responsibilities can I assume that will help accomplish them?"

8. He must cooperate with the meeting planners. If they need people to sit down front, he should sit down front. If they want discussion tables filled, he should not sit alone at a table toward the rear. If they ask for prompt starting times, he must observe them.

9. If a participant has a contribution to make, he should make it and make it clear and loud. If he simply wants to be seen and noted, he should cool it.

10. He should get out of the role of a sponge. A meeting is something not to be soaked up, but to get involved in.

11. Participants should avoid private side discussions. If his point is valid, a participant should share it with the group. If it is extraneous, he should keep quiet or leave the room to hold his private discussion.

Most participants have heard of management by objectives. If the meeting extends over several days, the following technique has been used with good results. Participants should be divided into groups of three to five. Management by objectives should be explained for those who may not be familiar with the concept. Then the following instructions should be given:

"Working individually, write a brief statement about your participation in this meeting—what would you identify as the three to five most important responsibilities you have as a participant?"

Individuals should be allowed to complete their work and then to discuss, in the small group, the responsibilities they have listed. The small group is then asked quickly to reach concensus on three to five responsibilities.

Each participant is then given one of the responsibilities and asked to complete a standard of performance for that responsibility. For example, if one of the responsibilities is group participation, the participant answers the question, "I will have satisfactorily performed the responsibility of group participation when . . ." He completes the statement.

The groups then report briefly on the responsibilities of the participants and the performance standards of each. The total group critiques the suggestions; this serves to set norms for the group. One responsibility usually identified is "I must listen". However, the standard for this responsibility can vary all over the lot. Some think the performance standard is simply to sit and look attentive. Others add they should take notes on significant items. Others think one should listen intently enough to be able to repeat back the heart of the presentation. Others think one has no responsibility if the material being presented is not applicable to that person. Still others believe one should be asking, "How can I use this in my small group or back home?" Still others feel the participant should be listening for what is not being said, errors in reasoning, use of faulty data, etc.

Some meeting planners ask different participants to assume different roles during the meeting. Part of the participants can be asked to pay special attention to the quality of the data used;

Figure 11.2. Behavior that will enable participants to achieve most from small group discussions.

---

1. The participant should participate in the discussion.
2. He should speak openly and freely.
3. He must listen to what others say—really listen. He must try to *understand* what they are saying. It is possible for another person to have a thought better than one's own idea.
4. He should help the discussion leader keep the discussion on the group task. If he sees the group straying from the subject, he should help bring them back.
5. He should sell his ideas to the group—not to the group leader.
6. He must keep his inputs short and to the point and the task.
7. If differences emerge, he must not avoid it or allow others to avoid it. Instead, he should identify the conflict, search for factual data and attempt to cope with the disagreement.
8. The participant must put his personal goals aside when these conflict with the group goals or the group process.
9. He should openly state his feelings when these feelings are relevant to the group's effective functioning. The group goal cannot include individual needs unless individual needs are expressed.
10. He must accept responsibility for what he says. He is responsible for the clarity of his communication and for its effect upon the group.
11. He must accept leadership or group support roles if the group asks him to do so or if he sees the need for them.

(Figure 11.2 continued on following page)

(Figure 11.2 continued)

12. If he does not understand something he should say
    so. The odds are strong that half the others do not
    understand, either.
13. Participants must have a basic respect for people and
    a willingness to recognize that every person is an im-
    portant individual entity.
14. They must identify with the group problems and act-
    ively seek group solutions.
15. They must be prepared to assist in carrying out group
    decisions.

another portion to think of questions others have but will not ask;
another part to summarize; another portion to look for job application; still another to look for concensus; etc.

As a participant in a meeting, a member has the kinds of
responsibilities listed in Figure 11.1.

In many meetings a participant will be placed in a small group
of five to eight other participants. Usually his group will be given a
task to accomplish. The kinds of behavior listed in Figure 11.2 will
enable the participant to get the most from these discussions and
to contribute maximally to the success of the meeting.

12
Meeting
Evaluation

Evaluation of the meeting is a constant concern of meeting planners. Periodically—about every five years—renewed attention is paid to the process. Additionally, when business declines, management and meeting sponsors anxiously ask, "Can you prove to me that meetings and educational activities pay off—I mean, in dollars and cents?" The literature abounds in attempts to do just this. The methodology is scientific, the terminology is professional and statistical and the percentage points are carried out to .0005. Few accept the results—not even the evaluator himself.

The effectiveness of meetings does need to be assessed, but the process is highly judgmental, many intervening variables intrude, and for the foreseeable future, the meeting planner is going to have to settle for rough guides as to his meetings' effectiveness. He may be in the position of a paper manufacturer to whom we once talked. This manufacturer monthly, in a metropolitan area, featured some aspect of his business. The displays were excellent, the ideas original and we often stopped by to look at the displays as did many others. On this occasion he was featuring not only his own products, but that of his competitors as well. From the look of the displays it was obvious they cost a great deal of money. He was asked whether the displays paid off financially. His frank answer was, "We don't know if they do or not—but we're afraid to stop them just in case they do." Evaluation of meetings is in about this same boat.

Most meeting planners know their meetings must be marketable. In these instances they are highly concerned with the participant happiness factor—"Did the participants enjoy the experience?" If they did, they will sign up for more. If they did not, the planner has a problem. The meeting planner more concerned with training and education knows happiness is not necessarily a good indicator of whether or not learning occurred. This planner is apt to take a more profound look at evaluation and not be swayed so readily by participant happiness.

Increasingly in recent years there has been an effort to correlate meeting objectives with evaluations. Ten years ago meeting objectives were globally stated and promised the impossible. Since they could not be evaluated, creature comforts—like, "Did you like the coffee?"—were evaluated. There is a tendency now to state objectives more simply and realistically. When this is done, the evaluation can more realistically gauge whether or not the meeting accomplished the objectives. This move is in quite the right direction.

Another factor has affected evaluations: there is a heightened awareness that learning comes at a high price. One can consider anything he knows and reflect how long it took him to learn that item, or one can observe the hours a mother spends teaching a toddler to say "Mama." Too often goals have been set, in a two to five day program, to radically change behavior, attitudes and values. This is sheer nonsense. Even if one could do it, he would question the personality integration of the participant. Attitudes, values and behavior change at a much slower pace and at a much higher price.

It is assumed that the meeting planner reading this book is most often not interested in a complex, highly sophisticated meeting evaluation. For those who are interested, a more in-depth discussion is included in this chapter. Most meeting planners, however, will simply be interested in a short immediately-after-the-program evaluation. For that reason a number of examples are included in the appendix.

The meeting planner needs to know what he wants to evaluate and why. If he understands this, the evaluation instrument almost writes itself. He can simply ask, "What do I want to know; what will I do with the information; and what do I need to ask to get this information?" The meeting planner may want information:

1. About how effectively the meeting objectives were met.
2. To determine if other new content should be added to similar programs; some content deleted or shortened; or other content expanded.
3. To determine if a follow-on program should be designed.
4. To use the data as a basis for follow-up activities.
5. To determine participant satisfaction with the facility, arrangements, mechanics, food, etc.
6. To determine participant acceptance of resource persons and speakers.
7. To secure suggestions about the methodologies used and the methodology "mix."
8. To determine other training or meeting needs the participants may have.
9. To determine if the level of information and content was too low, too high or just about right.
10. To determine if the time of the total program and subparts was adequate.
11. To determine the effectiveness and adequacy of visual aids.

The methods of evaluations can vary considerably. The most frequently employed are listed in Figure 12.1.

It is interesting to recall the history of evaluations within recent years. At first, meeting planners were only interested in a

Figure 12.1. Evaluation methods most frequently used.

1. A brief instrument containing a number of items and providing:
   a. A series of adjectives after each item being evaluated. The participant checks the adjective most closely describing his evaluation.
   b. A statement followed by a continuum. The participant checks the point on the continuum that most closely describes his evaluation. Thus, "How well did the meeting employ visual aids:"
2. Evaluation after each session or bloc of content.
3. Evaluation done periodically in the group—"pulse 'n temperature" sessions.
4. Reactor panels: members are selected at random from the participants. They sit in front of the rest of the participants and are interviewed as to how they evaluate the meeting.
5. File cards—5 by 8 inches. A plus (+) sign is placed on one side of the card, a minus(-) sign on the other. Participants are asked to comment on the plusses and minuses of the meeting.
6. Follow-up evaluation at local meetings back home.
7. Letters sent to the meeting planner by the participants instead of questionnaires.
8. Reports from those in supervisory positions over the participants.
9. Use of pre- and post-tests on knowledge and skills.
10. Faculty post-mortem.
11. An open-ended form. This can be as simple as asking what participants thought of the meeting. It may contain topic headings to direct the participant's thinking.

12. Tape recorders can be placed in two or three locations. Participants simply record their evaluation as things occur to them.
13. Selected participants can be briefed and meet with other participants to get their evaluations and report back to the steering group or to the meeting planner, or he can prepare a report. The interviews can be done with groups of participants in a formal setting or casually at mealtime or in other informal settings.
14. The meeting planners may depend upon their normal contacts and interviews with participants to provide the data they need.
15. The evaluation is usually conducted at the end of the meeting. Sometimes the meeting planner prefers to send the questionnaire form to the participants one to six weeks after they return home. The greatest problem here, of course, is that a number of participants will not return the questionnaire, and the meeting planners are not sure how those not responding felt about the meeting.

simple evaluation of the meeting. It usually dealt with the facility, creature comforts, interestingness of the meeting, entertainment value of the speakers, etc. It came to be known as the "happiness" rating. Later it became more sophisticated. It can be described as

Meeting . . . Evaluation.

As time went on, meeting planners found that, using such simple evaluations, the evaluation was very impressionistic. Most evaluators rated the last meeting as "the best I ever attended".

It also became apparent that participant entertainment was not synonymous with learning. Meeting planners discovered studies like the one that asked college students to rate instructors just as the student finished a course; then asked the student five years later to rate his instructors. Those professors who rated highest at the end of the course were seldom so rated five years later. The student, at the end of the course, tended to rate personality, jokes, easiness in grading, etc. Five years later, the student had discovered the "hard" professor who had good content and demanded the student's best was the one from whom the student had most often learned. Meeting planners became concerned whether participants found, after returning to their organization, that the meeting had been helpful to them performing more effectively on the job. Then follow-up evaluations began to be sent out, thus:

Meeting . . . Evaluation . . . Follow-up Evaluation

After a while some meeting planners felt that, to be more scientific, they should ascertain what the participants knew before they attended the meeting and what they knew after they attended the meeting. The following evolved:

Pretest . . . Meeting . . . Evaluation or Post-test

or

Pretest...Meeting...Evaluation or Post-test...Follow-up evaluation

Still later, in order to appear even more scientific, other meeting planners followed the format sketched in the above paragraph but now added a control group.

There, matters stood for a while, but the validity of the evaluations was still in question. In recent years, the following emphases have been added:

1. In order to evaluate performance and to design an effective program, the criteria of good performance on the job in this organization by the participants must be known. Much activity went into trying to determine what was considered good performance and the criteria. This is much more difficult to identify than most managers realize.
2. It was then suggested that this data should be used to set more limited and specific objectives for the program and the evaluation be used to test whether these objectives had been met.
3. With increased cost-profit squeezes in recent years, there has been even more questioning whether or not training can show a dollars-and-cents return. Efforts along the lines sketched above intensified.
4. Very recently there has been a disillusionment about evaluation and how discrete it can be—and with this an increased questioning as to whether or not meeting planners have promised too much could be attained during their meeting.

One of the problems that sometimes concerns the meeting planner is the question, "What can I do that will increase the possibility that the meeting will impact on the participant's behavior after he returns home or to the job?" Sometimes, of course, this is not a concern of the meeting planner. A number of devices have been employed to prolong the effect of a meeting. A listing of techniques that can be utilized for this purpose is given in Figure 12.2.

For those interested in a more in-depth treatment of evaluations, the following unpublished material is from a study made for a federal agency. Gratitude is acknowledged to Dr. James Owens, professor of business administration, the University of Maryland, who played a major role in the compilation of the information.

Figure 12.2. Techniques to increase meeting impact on participant's behavior.

1. A report of the meeting can be sent to the participants.
2. A copy of a particularly well received presentation can be sent to the participants.
3. Participants can be given a short, pertinent bibliography of books and/or articles readily available.
4. Supervisors back home should be encouraged to talk to the participant about his meeting experience and how some of it can be used on the job.
5. Participants should be encouraged to make reports back home.
6. A "gimmick" can be provided that can be taken home and be useful enough to enhance its probability of being retained; for example, a ruler with some concept, design, model, etc., on it that was the focal point of the meeting.
7. Summary of main points of the meeting, recommendations made by participants or other useful information to the meeting sponsors can be provided.
8. Some weeks after the meeting, a letter can be sent to participants asking them to state in what ways the meeting influenced their behavior or job after they returned.
9. A refresher program—usually one day in length—can be arranged some six months later.
10. An "alumnus" meeting can be planned before participants leave the meeting.
11. An article can be sent to participants each month.
12. A casette tape can be sent several weeks later containing some pertinent information.
13. A "memo to myself" can be used.
14. A conference telephone hook-up can be used for a refresher hour or two some weeks after the program.

The material is slanted toward the training professional, but it is also equally valid for the small meeting planner.

A System for Evaluating a Training Curriculum

Broadly speaking, the essence of the evaluation process is a comparison of participant's knowledge and performance skills before, and then after completion of, the program or any particular stage of it. The key question is: Where was the participant before the program, and where is he after the program? It can be noted that, in the main, it is the evaluation of the participants in a program that constitutes the evaluation of the program itself.

Much research over the past decade in the field of executive training has clarified and popularized an approach toward training often called the "systems approach." Essentially, the systems approach consists of clear determination and statement of the objectives sought, in terms of specific terminal behavior and knowledge; design of a program specifically aimed to produce the desired terminal behavior or knowledge; and finally, "feedback" (the evaluation process) to assess the extent to which the training program and curriculum produced this in the participants.

The word "test" recurs often in discussions of evaluation. Although a particular test, in content, method, structure and grading, will stand alone as a test to determine extent of competence in a particular knowledge or performance skill area, nevertheless all tests may be used for two distinct purposes:

1. To determine the current state of knowledge or performance skill in order to place or enter a participant in the appropriate stage of a curriculum;
2. To measure the extent to which a participant, after completing a particular stage of a program, has mastered the desired knowledge or performance skills constituting the objectives of that stage.

In the first case, tests can determine how much a participant knows and can do before he is entered into the program, thus enabling the program planner to enter the participant into the most appropriate stage of the curriculum. This avoids boring and sometimes demoralizing repetition of material the participant already knows or can handle. It also avoids wasteful investment of training funds and resources.

The second use of tests is the standard, and more familiar, function of measuring results achieved by participants during and at the completion of a program unit.

What is being tested is of supreme importance in the evaluation process. Three classifications of the objects of testing provide a framework for the discussion which follows:

1. *Testing Knowledge.* A particular stage of the meeting program might have as its objective to provide a particular body of knowledge. A test to determine whether a participant has successfully completed this stage will be a test of *knowledge.*
2. *Testing Performance Skills.* On the other hand, another stage of the training program might have as its objective to improve the ability of the participant to *do* something, such as communicate more persuasively. A test to determine how successfully a participant has completed this stage will be not of what he *knows* but of what he *can do*.
3. *Testing Value or Attitude Change.* This is by far the most difficult to assess. Often this is called behavior change. It is our contention that behavioral change does not necessarily mean there has been a change in attitudes or values. Since so much has been written in this area, it is not dealt with in depth in this discussion.

The principal emphasis in the evaluation of the program should be placed upon:

1. The evaluation of the participants themselves rather than the program as such, and
2. The *results* or *terminal behavior* of the participants in order to determine the actual, useful and practical effects which have been produced by means of the program. Essentially the program must be judged by means of evaluation of the *students*, its product.

The reason for conducting programs normally is better performance on the part of the participants. Hence the measure of success of the program is the measure of the *performance of the participants* after they have participated in it. This essentially is evaluation by results and is strongly recommended.

Much has been written about participant evaluation, and many designs for it attempted. These range from inexpensive post-meeting participant evaluations to elaborate, in-depth, multifaceted designs covering a period of two to three years and costing large amounts of money.

The results are not clear or consistent. Part of our difficulty is that we still do not really know how or why people learn. We know that it has something to do with motivation, with self-fulfillment drives, rewards and punishment, as perceived by the learner. Increasingly there is an awareness that one critical, neglected area is the work environment. People behave where they see the rewards. There is much evidence that training programs may be excellent, but they die on the vine if they are not accepted, supported, recognized or rewarded by the organization, peers, subordinates, bosses or recipients.

For these and other reasons, an increasing number of program planners and managements are relying on other indicators to evaluate programs. For example, such pragmatic statements and observations as "I don't know where he learned it—or how—or why; I just know he is now a better (or worse) employee."

We find that managers use the following kinds of pragmatic observations and performances to test the validity and value of training:

1. From interfacing organizations, comments that participants are easier to get along with than before the program.
2. A drop-off in complaint letters.
3. A better press.
4. Staff less resistant to change, more open-minded, more willing to experiment, better listeners and more innovative.
5. More favorable comment on the performance of staff than formerly.
6. Better staff work performed after training.
7. Potential recruits mention they have heard of the organization's training programs and were attracted by them.
8. Staff publish more articles in professional and popular journals.

Although *exact* measurement of the effects of programs is utopian, seldom can you find an organization that has dropped or severely curtailed their training activities that did not reinaugurate a training program within five years. The organization becomes painfully aware it is inbred, insufficiently aware of the technology and outside changing world, and in danger of becoming stagnant.

We know of no serious effort to explore or to use the above kinds of criteria in evaluating a curriculum or participants. We are inclined to think that the use of some of them, or similar criteria, may offer an avenue worthy of exploring and piloting as a means of evaluation.

In the development of methods and instruments, meeting planners must distinguish between the evaluation of:

1. Easily measured skills and knowledge which lend themselves to quantitative measurement, and
2. Intangibles that constitute much of the essence of any job.

Expectation of more than the art of evaluation now permits in either of these aforementioned categories can be as damaging as the failure of meeting planners to attempt any evaluation.

For example, highly quantitative methods and instruments applied to the evaluation of intangibles will usually be superficial and useless at best, and in many instances misleading, frustrating and injurious to both the goals of a program and the efforts to evaluate it. The proper attitude is that evaluation attempts must be made, but varying degrees of success and inherent limitations must be accepted if they are to be useful in a practical way.

Evaluation tests and procedures should be developed with some consultation, suggestions and recommendations from the participant group. They should be involved in order not only to introduce into the testing procedures a greater degree of realism but, most importantly, to improve the degree of their *genuine acceptance* of both the program and the evaluation.

Essentially, the task of evaluation is to evaluate terminal behavior. Nevertheless, because acceptance by the participants is of extreme importance, it is recommended that an evaluation form be developed, to be filled out by participants at the conclusion of each program, permitting them to express their *own* opinions, impressions and assessments of the benefit the training has been to them. Such an evaluation, although subjective and vulnerable to obvious bias, will serve to accomplish (inexpensively) two purposes:

1. Improvement of acceptance of the overall program by participants.
2. Feedback to curriculum planners concerning the participants' needs, expectations and desires, which can be useful in the process of redesigning the curriculum.

A principal dimension which should be continually considered by decision-making officials in a program potentially involving considerable cost is the *cost-benefit* aspect of the entire effort.

Since, as is generally true, all potential participants cannot be given an unlimited exposure to the program at the same time, carefully considered decisions must be made by meeting planners as to *how many* from *what* units representing *what regions* of the country and *what organizations* for *what quantity of hours* and *how soon* should be trained in terms of the maximum (marginal) cost-benefit to the overall organization for both the short and the long range.

In the interest of efficiency, with optimum utilization of funds allocated to programs and evaluation and cost minimizing, any test can and should be used for a variety of purposes. Any single test, once designed, developed and established for use with standard procedures and forms, can be used (at little additional cost) to:

1. Determine the current status of a participant's knowledge and skills in order to *enter* him into the most appropriate stage, level or "track" within the training curriculum;
2. Determine the current status of a participant's knowledge and skills when he has completed a particular part of the curriculum in order to grade him as to his degree of success or failure in mastering the material;

3. Determine the current status of a participant's retention of knowledge and skills, periodically, in order to *rate* him for performance and/or promotion and salary increases;

4. Determine the current status of a participant in order to enter him in a "trained readiness" roster.

Some attempt should be made to surmount the validity and reliability problems in testing. The sponsoring office should be confident that the tests or evaluations are actually measuring what they are supposed to. At a minimum, perhaps, a systematic check could be made of a sample of the trainees to check the *consistency* between test data, interviews, performance measures, the resume, the field analysis and other evaluation data on the *same* individual.

The important question being raised here is to what extent does the test date predict the value of the criterion, i.e., some measure of successful performance?

The following methods are most commonly employed to evaluate the effectiveness of training and programs:

Pre- and Post-Testing

Wherever feasible and appropriate, in terms of the kind of thing being measured and the *cost* of measuring, it is recommended that the method of *pre- and post-testing* be used, with a control group, as the ideal method of evaluating the results of a training program. Pre- and post-testing involves testing, using random samples, a group of trainees and thus comparing their knowledge, skills or performance *before* and *after* the program.

This ideal method of testing, in many instances, will *not* be feasible or realistic in terms of the intangible thing being measured and/or disproportionate cost involved.

When a need for evaluation presents itself, it should be formulated in researchable terms and reduced to a practical scope in time and cost. The data required must be defined, and the possibility of translating findings into action within the organization should be ascertained. An "ideal" method of evaluation might include the following:

1. As indicated before, the only truly effective program is one which causes (measurably?) favorable changes in performance after the trainee returns to his job. The assertation is valid. A major dimension of any projected evaluation must, therefore, measure such changes. A "before" and "after" behavior profile would be obtained.

2. The highest level in relevance and quality comes about with use of objective performance scores. These scores may be determined either for the participant or for his subordinates. It is generally considered to be stronger evidence if the effectiveness is not only on the part of the participant, but on the part of his subordinates and associates as well. However, there are several dangers in the objective performance scores. Perhaps the most important is bias in the measures, that is, the influence to some unknown degree of factors other than the participant's contribution to the organization.

3. A comparison of relevant point of view of trainee's on-the-job behavior would be secured. (Reality is what it is perceived to be by the perceiver.) What is the "reality" of the pre-training and post-training behavior of the program participants? A sample of the perceptions of various populations would be necessary to get at the "truth." Among these will be those of the superior, the pregroup, the subordinates and perhaps the second-removed echelon of superiors and subordinates. In addition, what does the organization feel is most important in improved performance?

    It is desirable to sample the post-training opinions and feelings and the trainee himself over a period of time and in a variety of ways. These opinions can be useful as indications of acceptance of the training by participants, but they hardly provide extremely reliable and valid measures of factors, such as increase of knowledge, skills and performance. Structured rating scales which focus attention upon specific factors usually provide somewhat more reliable measures, but they still measure opinions. These are much more difficult to construct and obtain, but the increased confidence which can be placed in results may warrant the increased effort of measurement.

4. Doubtless the greatest methodological difficulty lies in finding ways of either validating or relaxing the "ceteria paribus" assumption. All things are not equal, particularly to ongoing organizational situations. Ways need to be devised so that reasonable assurance of fairly reliable cause-effect ascriptions can be made.

Evaluation of training could include a series of "research in depth" analyses. The principal purposes would be to provide (a) a basis for ascertaining the extent to which the general evaluation methodology is not uncovering relevant dimensions of trainee attitudinal and behavioral change, and (b) a check upon the cause-and-effect ascriptions suggested by the general evaluation data.

The output of such interviews is the joint product of the interviewer's and the respondent's interaction. The respondent usually communicates only when he feels it to his advantage. An extrinsic or negative motive lies in the possibility of a checkup on facts. There is also an intrinsic motivation in the satisfaction felt by most respondents in having an opportunity to converse on a basis of empathy. The interviewer must think about what the other person is saying and why, rather than about how he will phrase the following questions. At the same time, the interviewer has to direct the conversation so that content will meet the objectives. The questions must be keyed in wording to the overlap of the respondent's frame of language with that of the interviewer's objectives. The respondent's frame of reference (personal experience) in use of words can be revealed by the reasons he gives for his answers.

There would be a sample of several "control" groups (comprised of trainees not enrolled in the training programs) in order to check the research methodology and data in various ways and to determine a yardstick in terms of which to measure the degree of objective achievement of the training program.

The determination of the size of the sample is one of the most difficult problems facing an evaluator. Many novices attempt to start their project with the determination of the amount of "work" they will have to do instead of planning to solve a problem, regardless of the work entailed. Admittedly, it is often necessary to be "practical" and attempt to get the best answers possible with the least amount of effort.

It is easy to say that the sample should be adequate and representative of the population, but "adequate" and "representative" are ambiguous terms. It would be preferable to say that the proper size of a sample depends partly on the purpose of the study and partly on the nature of the population studied. For a placement into a type and level of training program, each participant would have to be tested or rated. For evaluation of training program results, however, a sample of the population may be chosen. Ordinarily, the sampling error or, in general terms, the amount of variation that may be attributed to change elements, varies inversely as the square root of a number of cases drawn in the sample. That is, we would expect to find about twice as much sampling error in a sample of a given size as we would in one four times as large.

In general, the more variation that exists in the population with respect to a characteristic being investigated, the larger the sample ought to be. If information is available about this characteristic from previous studies of the population, various sampling error formulas may be obtained. The characteristic being examined, for example, might be the amount of knowledge about certain technical material.

From a logical point of view, the size of a sample should be dependent upon the extent to which the individuals are representative of the population to be studied, the inclusiveness of the sample, the types of groups involved, the number of categories of data required and the method of analysis of the data. It is absolutely essential that the size of the total sample be large enough to permit valid analyses of subsamples used in the smallest breakdown of information to be made. In order that the smallest breakdown of information be representative, there must be fairly large number of cases in the subsample (25 to 30 would be the minimum as a "rough rule of thumb") instead of only three or four. Thus, this minimum number for each small breakdown could be multiplied by the number of subcategories, etc., for an estimate of the total sample. However, this process assumes that a random selection of cases in each subcategory will be uniform throughout the population—an assumption that does not hold for many human characteristics of populations. Probably, the evaluator should plan for a size of sample somewhat larger than this process would indicate to insure a satisfactory number of cases in the smallest category.

Paper and Pencil Testing

Little need be said about the advantages of this technique. For the purposes of rapidly, inexpensively and promptly learning the extent to which the participant has acquired knowledge, this test has no equal.

The paper and pencil test is most appropriate for determining the extent to which a participant has absorbed and understood technical material. There are several types of paper and pencil tests:

1. Short answer items (completion or direct question):
    a. Advantages:
        (1). Minimizes guessing.
        (2). Relatively easy to construct.
        (3). Familiar and natural to the examinee.
        (4). Easier to grade than essay, case or simulation exercise.
    b. Disadvantages:
        (1). More difficult and time consuming to score than other types of objective test items.
        (2). Demands only recall of information, rather than application and generalization.
        (3). Participants may complain of unfairness and ambiguity in questions.
        (4). Motivates students to study simply to recall factual information.

c. When to use:
   (1). Particularly useful in program and technical information where results of complex reasoning processes can be represented by a few symbols or words.
   (2). Check knowledge portions of public administration and management and public community relations.
   (3). Wherever essay questions are applicable.

d. Administration:
   (1). Can be administered by participants themselves. Results perhaps would only be used for self-development. Possibility of cheating, but this kind of administration might help to build trust and confidence in the system.
   (2). Can be administered fairly easily by staff as an evaluation and classification scheme.

2. Multiple choice or sequential testing
   a. Advantages:
      (1). Logical development of knowledge demanded in questions.
      (2). May require interpretation, seeing or understanding relationships.
      (3). Allows testing from application of the facts and principles in new situation.
      (4). Minimizes guesing.
   b. Disadvantages:
      (1). Difficult to construct.
      (2). Participants may complain of unfairness and ambiguity in questions.
      (3). Situation descriptions may need to be quite long, thus reducing testing time per amount of material.
   c. When to Use:
      (1). To measure participant's understanding.
      (2). To determine participant's ability to apply facts and principles to new situations.
      (3). To check knowledge of program policy and technical information.
   d. Administration: Same as short answer.

3. Matching items
    The trainee is instructed to place in front of each statement in
    the first column a letter preceding the word or phrase in the
    second column that is most closely associated to it.
    a. Advantages:
        (1). Can measure large amounts of factual information with
             relatively short expenditure of testing time.
        (2). Can measure association of events with participant's
             actions.
        (3). Easy to score.
    b. Disadvantages:
        (1). Difficult to construct.
        (2). Terminology limits plausible but wrong responses.
        (3). Motivates trainee to study factually.
        (4). Participants may complain of unfairness and ambiguity
             in questions.
    c. When to Use:
        (1). To test for factual knowledge, association and applica-
             tion of information.
        (2). To check knowledge of program, policy and technical
             information.
    d. Administration: Same as short answer.

Observation Tests

Observation can be very useful in the evaluation of many phases and
aspects of the training curriculum and its intended results. A test of this
type would consist of a trained person, such as someone from the training staff or an outside consultant, observing the performance of a participant either on the job or in simulations where the extent of his knowledge and skill in performance of his job would be evident.

Oral Testing

Oral testing has many advantages in determining the true knowledge
and ability which is at the instantaneous command of the participant.

The Essay-Type Test

The writing of an essay still constitutes one of the most demanding exercises which a human being can master, as well as a most revealing indicator of competence. To cite a simple example, a participant in the program could be asked, at the end of a particular day, to draft an essay to be presented by him the next day, on the principal application that he sees to his own job of the somewhat theoretical material which was dealt with. His essay, turned out in response to this request, would be a most revealing indication of the extent to which he understood and was able to apply the material which had been covered.

The same procedure could be used in the form of a request, at any given time, of a participant to report on certain aspects of his job. His report clearly and distinctly would, in most cases, reveal his true understanding and grasp of the nature of his job. It might be noted that the *essay* approach to evaluation is a relatively inexpensive one on the part of the person being evaluated. It is a technique understandably used consistently in universities at both the undergraduate and graduate levels.

These tests can be essays, simulation such as case problems or in-basket exercises. The administration of this type of test would probably have to be by the staff or others such as consultants. The advantages and disadvantages of these types of subjective written tests are quite similar. Thus we will discuss the essay test first and then point out any advantages or disadvantages unique to the case or in-basket approach.

The essay test is highly regarded by many trainers and educators; it is strongly criticized by others. The fact that it has remained in use despite such criticism testifies to its utility. Its continuance is based largely on the fact that it is regarded as capable of measuring "the higher mental processes involved in selecting and organizing ideas, formulating and supporting hypotheses, logically developing an argument, and writing creatively." Despite the weight of evidence concerning the low reliability of the scoring, essay tests cannot be ignored. Trainers have begun to see more clearly that the validity is the overriding consideration. A test, to be valid, must be relevant as well as reliable. And the written essay, composed by the participant-trainee within boundaries laid down by the trainer who frames the question, is frequently the most relevant measure.

Trainees often criticize essay tests on the grounds that questions are poorly phrased and framed, and often these criticisms are valid. One of the advantages of the essay test—the freedom of response permitted the student—may also be a great handicap if too much freedom is allowed. In general, it is wise to provide at least some structure and boundary to essay questions.

A sample of a relatively narrow portion of the trainees' true knowledge of subject is attained. This disadvantage may be overcome to an extent by including a large number of questions, each requiring a brief answer, rather than merely a few requiring extensive answers.

The problem of low reliability in the scoring of essay tests is usually high on the list of criticisms. Experienced evaluators, however, are able to at least partially overcome this problem through a variety of controls such as a check list of factors, determination of scoring on a relative basis, etc.

The Field Analysis

An acid-test type of evaluation, which can occasionally be used to judge the progress and status of a participant is the field analysis. This would consist of a participant being requested to visit an organization other than his own and to analyze the strengths and deficiencies of it in the form of a written report, copies of which would be made available to the curriculum planners and the evaluators of the program. This particular technique, happily a relatively inexpensive one, confronts the participant with an actual situation, his analysis and report of which will reveal rapidly and clearly his overall grasp of his job as well as his own personal strengths and weaknesses. It might be noted that this technique of field analysis is as valuable a method of training as it is of evaluation. There may be some resistance to this approach on the part of those who are participants in the area subject to investigation. They might resent careful scrutiny of their local program by an "outsider" who makes a short visit and may not really understand the situation.

Evaluation by Resource Person

Evaluation by a resource person can be a useful method which, in terms of cost-benefit, is desirable because of its simplicity. Certainly at the conclusion of an entire stage of the program, and possibly at the conclusion of certain of its phases, the resource person could be asked, by requesting him to complete certain prearranged forms, to comment on the results, knowledge, skills and ability of individual participants. Since the resource person is there anyway, it requires very little additional effort on his part to enter evaluations which occur to him at the moment and which can be extremely useful to the organization. It should be noted that this sort of evaluation is utilizing techniques involving observations, interview, etc. However, many training and program sponsors believe this method violates some of the basic principles of learning, such as willingness to risk or to try new behavior.

Counseling and Guidance

Counseling and guidance, and an orderly procedure for providing these, should constitute a significant, if indirect, part of the overall evaluation process. Guidance and counseling provide simultaneously a vehicle for determining a man's development goals as well as partial evaluation of the extent to which he is successfully reaching these goals.

The Performance Commitment Approach

Another valuable and inexpensive method of evaluation is the performance commitment approach. This involves the joint determination by the participant and his immediate superior of the goals (in terms of results) which both he and his superior *agree* are feasible over a stated period of time. This commitment, on the part of the participant, obviously constitutes a standard against which, at a later time, he can be measured in terms of results. Most importantly, the standard against which he is to be measured is one which *he* accepts in his performance *commitment* (which avoids the usual problem in appraisal of the person feeling that he is being appraised by means of standards which are unfair and which have never been accepted by him.)

The performance commitment approach requires a high degree of rapport and mutual trust between superior and subordinate.

Simulation Techniques

Simulation techniques, such as games, case studies, in-basket exercises, incidents, role playing, problem confrontations, etc., should be used as often as is appropriate to the training or program design (insofar as these techniques contribute directly to the training curriculum itself). The simulation techniques mentioned should be incorporated into the curriculum *primarily* as a training device; however, these same techniques can, secondarily, be used as an excellent method of *evaluating* the extent to which certain knowledges, skills, and abilities to perform are being realized on the part of participants. In order to accomplish this secondary purpose, in the use of these techniques it is necessary only to develop certain simple forms which can be filled out at the completion of the simulation exercise on which forms competent trainers, acting also as evaluators, can indicate their appraisal of the knowledge, skills or ability to perform of the participants.

Case analysis suffers from the same disadvantages as the essay approach. However, it may be considered a further step toward relevance or validity in the testing instrument.

The study and analysis of cases follow essentially the same steps that a participant would use in resolving an actual problem. There are some differences in emphasis, however, so a brief summary of the technique of the case study and analysis may be helpful. Participants (a) develop a clear mental picture of the situation being studied; (b) clarify the problem orally or in writing; (c) determine the alternatives and the key factors in deciding which is best; (d) organize and analyze the facts; (e) decide on the course of action; (f) check the decision from several angles; and (g) prepare an appropriate recommendation or instruction.

The participant's case analysis would be judged on several criteria such as adequacy, balance, validity, reasonableness of interpretations, objectivity, thoroughness of reasoning, perspective, detail of development and consequences of proposed actions.

Other simulation techniques consist of games, in-basket, incident, role playing, problem confrontation and other such devices which simulate in a classroom or laboratory setting the actual job, or part of the job which the participant performs. The chief advantage of this method is its similarity to the actual job. It has the advantage of concrete reality as distinct from comfortable distraction. The chief disadvantages, of course, are the amount of time that is required to properly conduct it, and the fact that all the variables, information and organization totality and realism cannot be captured or included.

In the in-basket approach, as an example of simulation testing, the trainee is presented with a "basket" of letters, memos, notices, etc., and within a time limit, asked for detailed information on his courses of action for each item and *why*.

A number of games, manual and computerized, have been developed in recent years. Most of these are "time compressed" and provide immediate feedback to participants. The use of video tape has increasingly come into use for evaluation of certain kinds of behavior—for example, interviewing, sales closing, etc. These are not discussed here because of their complexity and also because they are widely written up in the literature.

Simulation provides for realism in testing for particular important aspects of the participant's job. An indication of his skill in supervision, management and public relations may be developed. In general, the simulation approach has the same advantages and disadvantages as the essay testing and case analysis. That is, for example, the problem of low reliability in the scoring may be present.

Standard Evaluation Forms and Procedures

Efforts can be made by the sponsoring training or program office to establish a system of standard procedures and forms for the purpose of evaluations in various aspects of the participant's job where they could be conveniently completed, in writing, by the many officials who deal with them. For example, such a form appropriately designed, could be regularly submitted to persons who deal with the participant, and who, by means of the form, could give their opinion of the competence of the participant in terms of certain specifically named knowledges, skills or performances which constitute his job. This technique would primarily involve a certain ingenuity in developing a form which would provide the information desired and a method of persuading such interfacing persons of the benefits which would accrue to them as they participate each year or period in its completion.

Evaluating Attitudes

Attitude is of considerable importance. Although any method of evaluation of attitude will be subjective at best, some effort should be made to assess this very important, although intangible, dimension of the successful participant. Such an assessment will necessarily be done, almost exclusively, by some indication of the attitudes of the participant, including himself.

It is noted that the subjective evaluation is still an essential method. Many job aspects are simply immeasurable in any quantitative way and, therefore, the subjective opinions of competent persons who deal regularly with the participant to be appraised constitute a most valuable assessment of his knowledge, skills and ability to perform. The personnel folders of people abound in this kind of evaluation which, despite its obvious limitations, is useful, inexpensive and a method definitely to be used.

Rating

Consideration should be given to systems of rating, such as the critical incident technique, graphic rating scale, rank order, forced distribution, forced choice, performance against written standards, etc., in terms of costs and problems involved compared to value expected. The critical incident technique should receive special attention as a device useful for several purposes such as evaluation of participants, gaining involvement in the training program, providing realism, establishing priorities in content and sequence of the training activities, etc.

There are numerous devices used in this rating. The graphic rating-scale method is the most frequently used. With this method the person doing the rating puts a check mark on a form next to a word or phrase describing the degree of merit for each of several different traits such as "quality of work," "quantity of work," "cooperation," etc. Degrees of merit might run from "inadequate" to "superior," "below average" to "above average," etc. A major problem with graphic rating scales is that such words as "superior," or "average," etc. mean different things to different people. The traits themselves, e.g., "cooperation," "loyalty," etc., are subject to a different interpretation. These problems can be minimized by training of raters and using descriptive statements to explain the various degrees on each trait scale.

Another device of traditional merit rating is the rank-order method, in which all of the participants to be rated by a superior (or by peers or subordinates) are ranked from best to poorest in one or more traits. If groups to be rated differ in size, statistical corrections need to be made to compare the relative standing of individuals in one group with that of those in another.

Another rating technique is the forced distribution method, in which the individuals rated are distributed along one or more scales, and a fixed percentage (say one-third) of the participants are assigned to the best and worst ends of the scale and to the middle bracket. This method is similar to the teaching technique of "grading on the curve."

Another method which can be used in conjunction with those above is the critical incident technique. This technique involves keeping a record of unusually good or undesirable incidents occurring in a participant's work perhaps before and then after the training program. It provides a factual record for ratings, for subsequent discussions in training programs and for decision making. A danger in this method, of course, is the possibility that the superior may accumulate a number of bad incidents and may unload them on the participant all at one time with negative repercussions. The superior may also neglect to discuss the incidents at the time of the occurrence when discussion would be the most meaningful.

A forced-choice rating method has also come into some use; it features a series of descriptive statements in sets of four, with the rater choosing the most descriptive and least descriptive statements from each set. This method appears to minimize the "halo effect" problem and of different interpretation of the meaning of points on trait scales. The "halo effect" is the tendency for the rater to rate a person high on every trait if the person is outstanding in one particularly desirable characteristic and to rate low on all traits if there is some particularly conspicuous undesirable characteristic.

A second major rating system is the comparison of performance measures against written standards. However, the use of performance standards does not eliminate the need for the more traditional kind of rating. Some traditional form of rating must still be used to make comparisons between participants for purposes of placement into specific training program levels and types. Or, to say it another way, conclusions still must be drawn about the implications of the discrepancies or congruencies between standards and achievement. Comparing performance standards against actual performance may increase objectivity in arriving at these placement decisions, but the decisions as to relative ranking still remain to be made.

Although most rating systems involve superiors rating subordinates, and probably most people prefer this arrangement, peer ratings and ratings by subordinates have been used with effectiveness in a few situations. The judgment of additional people, who in some cases may have more intimate knowledge, is brought to bear on the problem. The major problem, however, in the use of peer or subordinate ratings is the potential danger that the ratings may be made on the basis of performance which is useful to the rater but not necessarily to the organization.

The introduction of administrative procedures for rating participants may force modifications in the organizational system. The procedures may work to some degree, but rather less well than the organization might desire and with some complications. Research and consulting experience indicates that the rating system may yield:

1. Widespread antagonism to the rating system and to those who administer it.
2. Successful resistance and beating the system.
3. Unreliable performance information because of 1 and 2 above.
4. The necessity for a close surveillance.
5. High administrative cost.

Summary

Evaluation is one of the most difficult and exasperating functions management performs. In large part, the exasperation arises because management feels convinced that good management requires exact evaluation of efforts made and, at the same time, it has experienced the virtual impossibility of exact evaluation.

Let it be noted again that expectation of more than the art of evaluation now permits can be as damaging as the failure of management to attempt evaluation at all.

Research in the field of evaluation constantly confirms the principle that the evaluator must judge results rather than methods used. Curriculum and meeting planners can easily become obsessed with the intrinsic beauty and neatness of their structure and methodology; however, the purpose of the curriculum is *results* in terms of better performance on the part of participants.

Many approaches to training seem to be accepted as desirable on the basis of face validity. The objectives appear desirable and the methods employed seem workable. However, face validity is not sufficient in the evaluation of training activities; a somewhat more objective evaluation is required. Careful consideration of these activities would serve several purposes as indicated before. First, considerable cost is involved in many of these activities. There is a need to determine whether or not the results justify this expense. Furthermore, objective evaluation of the many different training approaches would facilitate the choice of techniques most appropriate for given needs. And finally, precise evaluation of training activities would identify the more and the less effective aspects of each and thus contribute to their improvement.

Evaluation involves measurement of results and comparison with a predetermined standard. Evaluation sought in training is basically similar to that sought for other management practices—how effectively and efficiently are the desired results attained? The actual procedure for evaluation can be quite involved, however, and one should bear in mind several cautions and considerations.

The objectives sought in training must be defined operationally in such a manner that they can be measured. Criteria for the evaluation must be specified, measures of these criteria developed, and procedures for measurement and comparison must be developed. All of these factors determine the validity of the usefulness of the evaluation.

Three basic levels for evaluation are found in current practice. The first of these focuses attention upon the level of achievement of objectives upon completion of training activities; criterion measures are obtained after the training has been completed. This approach indicates the degree to which objectives have been achieved, but it does not indicate the change in achievement *associated with training*; it provides no indication of the increase in achievement of objectives.

A second approach involves measurement both *before* and *after* the completion of the training. The evaluation of training is by means of the trained group only. This is not an ideal experimental design. It is, however, widely used and better than no evaluation at all, assuming that adequate criterion measures and analysis procedures are employed.

A third (and more ideal) approach is the controlled experimental study. The procedure is as follows: (a) a "before" proficiency measure is taken for both a control and an experimental group; (b) one group is trained while the other is left on the job; (c) an "after" proficiency measure is taken for both groups; (d) the "before" is subtracted from the "after" for both groups to measure the gain in proficiency. The control group should receive, so far as possible, as much attention (exclusive of training) as the trained group. Odd as it may seem, it is not at all uncommon for the control group to gain as much as the trained group in job proficiency.

There are a number of problems which emerge in using measurement instruments or procedures. The foremost among these are the validity and reliability problems. Probably the most common deficiency in evaluation program in organizations is the lack of knowledge about the validity of the procedures that are being used. Far too often assumptions are made about what the tests and procedures are doing, but there is no attempt to verify these. Sometimes tests are used which have been validated in other situations; but unless the organization is confident that its situation is very similar, no one can be sure what the test is measuring. Even if the situations appear very similar, there can be some doubt.

From a statistical standpoint, validity is the extent to which a test *predicts* the value of a criterion. Statistical validity refers to the correlation between a predictor and a criterion measure. The criterion is a measure of some degree of success in performance. Ordinarily, in industrial and government testing, validity means the extent to which a test will predict some criterion of job "success," although criteria such as attendance or turnover records are sometimes used. The most common mistake, then, is the use of a test or procedure without knowledge of how accurately it predicts job performance.

The selection of a criterion is a big problem in itself. That is, "what is meant by success," if that is what we want to predict? A number of complexities are immediately encountered. For example, if we use ratings by officials as a criterion of success, are the ratings of the various officials comparable, or does one rate his employees high and the other rate his employees low? How reliable are the ratings of an individual official? Do raters evaluating the same people know them equally well? If we use an objective measure, to what degree is this measure related to contributing to goals of the operation? All of these are problems in determining an appropriate criterion of success. This is probably the most difficult problem in evaluation.

Once the criterion scores are obtained, statistical validation requires the computation of the correlation between test scores and criterion scores. The correlation coefficient becomes the measure of validity. Once this coefficient is computed, statements as to the probability of success, given different test scores, can be calculated.

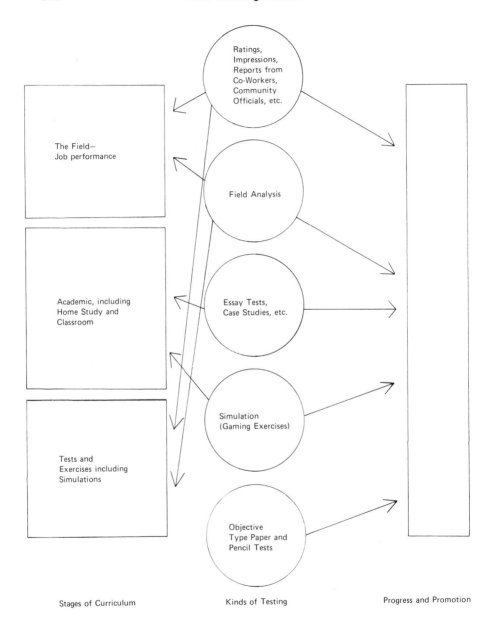

Ratings,
Impressions,
Reports from
Co-Workers,
Community
Officials, etc.

The Field—
Job performance

Field Analysis

Academic, including
Home Study and
Classroom

Essay Tests,
Case Studies, etc.

Simulation
(Gaming Exercises)

Tests and
Exercises including
Simulations

Objective
Type Paper and
Pencil Tests

Stages of Curriculum   Kinds of Testing   Progress and Promotion

Figure 12.3. One possible approach toward a matrix for utilization of an evaluation system.

In addition to statistical validation, there is also clinical validation. In this the test scores are used in conjunction with as many other data about the person taking the test as can reasonably be obtained. For example, it might be judged that a participant with a Master's degree in public administration might not need certain portions of the training program. In our opinion, test data should always be used in conjunction with information obtained from the resume, the interview and other sources. Through such "cross validation," the highest validity can be obtained.

Closely related to the problem of validity is the matter of reliability which is the extent to which test results are consistent. In a validation there have been three traditional ways of determining some indication of reliability: (a) the repeat of a test or the retest method; (b) the alternate form method (given a second form of the test to see if similar results are obtained); (c) the split-half method. In each method a correlation coefficient is computed to determine the degree of consistancy.

If a test is unreliable—if it measures inconsistently—validity is bound to be relatively low. If the accuracy of the test score cannot be relied upon, the statistics which relate test scores to the criterion cannot be relied upon.

The eternal question arises as to the distinction between the evaluation of a curriculum and the evaluation of the students exposed to it. On this point, we take a strong position: essentially, the curriculum must be judged by means of evaluation of the students, its products. The reason for the curriculum is better performance on the part of the participants. Hence, the measure of success of the curriculum is that of the *performance* of the students after they have participated in it. Again, this is evaluation by *results*.

Although, in its essential purposes, a curriculum can be judged best by evaluating the students who complete it, there is *one* aspect which can and should be evaluated somewhat *independently* of the *student* performance. And this is the relationship of costs to a (planned) expectation of certain "target" results. [Figure 12.3 illustrates the interrelationships among an employee's job performance responsibilities and tasks, his progress through the organization and the various forms of evaluations discussed.]

It is better to know nothing
than to know what ain't so.

H.W. Shaw (1884) (Josh Billings)

13

Reference Aids

From time to time the meeting planner has need for information that is not easily available. It was hoped that a number of these items could be included in this chapter, but the source of much of the material is not in the public domain. Further, to include all of the things the meeting planner occasionally needs would have exceeded the number of pages this book was designed to meet.

The meeting planner will find it extremely useful to use a notebook, with appropriate tabs, for this purpose. As appropriate materials, or their sources, are located, he can place them in the notebook. Such a resource can save hours of fruitless search when the data is needed.

The following are a few suggestions for locating some of the data infrequently needed but difficult to locate when the need arises.

Forms of Address

Almost any good secretarial handbook will contain information on forms of address. It is especially useful when addressing, or writing, people such as ministers, political figures, officials, foreign dignitaries, etc.

Seating Protocol

Information on seating protocol is not often used by the small meeting planner but can create uneasy moments when needed. The best resources found are government, city or organizational personnel whose functions require this special knowledge. Any references seen tend to deal only with certain kinds of guests—for example, foreign political figures. Local resources whose jobs encompass these kinds of responsibilities are the best resources.

Holidays

A good calendar clearly showing all holidays is indispensable. A few are published that are three- to five-year calendars, and these can be most helpful. Fortunately, most of these are free. A few inquiries among friends and businesses will locate two or three such calendars. A large calendar for the current year, with space for each day that allows for penciled notes, is a parallel "must."

Display of the Flag

Good resources for information on the appropriate way to display the flag, when displayed alone or in conjunction with other flags, can be found in:

1. *Our flag.* Office of Armed Forces Information and Education. Department of Defense. (Also pictures all the 50 state flags). House Document 165. Available from the Government Printing Office. 25 cents.

2. *How to Respect and Display our Flag.* U.S. Marine Corps.
    NAVMC 5901 PB (Revised 1948).
3. Public Law 829. 77th Congress. Chapter 806—2d Session.

Parliamentary Procedure

On occasion the meeting planner will find need for some of
the simpler parliamentary procedures. Appreciation is expressed to
the League of Women Voters of the United States for the following parliamentary procedures.*

Principal Motions

General Statement: When a motion has been made, seconded and
stated by the chair, the assembly is not at liberty to consider any other
business until this motion has been disposed of. If the motion is long and
involved, the chairman asks the mover to hand it in writing to the secretary. The mover cannot withdraw his motion after it has been stated by
the chair. In general all important motions should be seconded, which
may be done without rising or addressing the chair.

1. To Amend: This motion is "to change, add, or omit words" in
    the original main motion, and is debatable, majority vote.
    To Amend the Amendments: This is a motion to change, add,
    or omit words in the first amendments; debatable, majority
    vote.
    Method: The first vote is on changing words of second amend-
    ment, the second vote (if first vote adopts change) on first
    amendment as changed; the third vote is on adopting main mo-
    tion as changed.

*The League of Women Voters of the United States, *Simplified Parliamentary
Procedure,* Section IV (Washington, D.C.).

2. To Commit: When a motion becomes involved through amendments or when it is wise to investigate a question more carefully, it may be moved to commit the motion to a committee for further consideration. Debatable—Amendable—Committee must make report on such question.

3. To Lay on the Table: The object of this motion is to postpone the subject under discussion in such a way that it can be taken up at some time in the near future when a motion "to take from the table" would be in order. These motions are not debatable or amendable: majority vote.

4. To Postpone: A motion to postpone the question before the assembly to some future time is in order, except when a speaker has the floor. Debatable: majority vote.

5. To adjourn: This motion is always in order except:

   a. When a speaker has the floor.
   b. When a vote is being taken.
   c. After it has just been voted down.
   d. When the assembly is in the midst of some business which cannot be abruptly stopped.

   Under all the above circumstances, the motion is not debatable. When the motion is made to adjourn to a definite place, and time, it is debatable.

6. To Reconsider: The motion to reconsider a motion that was carried or lost is in order if made on the same day or the next calendar day, but must be made by one who voted with the prevailing side. No question can be twice reconsidered. Debatable: majority vote.
   Requires 2 votes: First on whether it should be reconsidered. Second on original motion after reconsideration.

7. The Previous Question: Is to close debate on the pending question. This motion may be made when debate becomes long

drawn out. It is not debatable. The form is "Mr. (Madam) Chairman, I move the previous question." The chairman then asks, "Shall debate be closed and the question now be put?" If this be adopted by a two-thirds vote, the question before the assembly is immediately voted upon.

8. Point of Order: This motion is always in order, but can be used only to present an objection to a ruling of the chair or some method of parliamentary procedure. The form is "Mr. (Madam) Chairman, I rise to a point of order." The Chairman: "Please state your point of order." After the member has stated his objection, the chair answers:

    a. "Your point of order is sustained" or
    b. "Your point of order is denied."

    If any member is not satisfied he may appeal from the decision of the chair. The chairman then addresses the assembly, "Shall the decision of the chair be sustained?" This is debatable and the presiding officer may discuss it without leaving the chair. Voted on like any other motion: majority or tie vote sustains the decision of chair. Requires a majority of "no" votes to reverse decision of the chair.

14
Boards and Committees

As one talks to people who are serving on the boards and committees of voluntary and nonprofit organizations, it becomes apparent that many of these people are disenchanted with their roles. The most common complaint is "I really don't do anything that challenges me or that makes me feel I am providing a worthwhile service. All the board does is listen to the minutes, the treasurer's report, and reports of committees—and then rubber-stamp the recommendations of either the committee or the paid director."

This chapter is primarily directed to those small meeting planners who must plan and/or conduct board and committee meetings of voluntary and nonprofit organizations. In recent years a great deal of attention has been directed to boards and committees in business and industry. Many of the factors dealt with in that context are also applicable to voluntary and nonprofit organizations. Conversely, most of this chapter is also applicable to the private sector. However, there has been less written to identify the special problems confronting the planner of meetings of boards and committees in voluntary and nonprofit organizations. It is the intent of this chapter to help these planners.

Most board and committee members of voluntary and nonprofit organizations are not specialists or professionals in the field of work of the organization. In the private sector the reverse tends to be true. For the voluntary and nonprofit organizations this was done intentionally. Initially, the major functions of such boards and committees were representation of the community views, major policy development, supervision of the paid executive, public relations, and helping the organization's fund-raising efforts.

Increasingly the job has become more complex. Some organizations are operating multimillion dollar budgets; the technologies involved in the business are highly complex; decisions must be made in the milieu of a complicated community and national structure; and boards and committees increasingly are being held legally liable for their actions and decisions.

As a result, many such organizations are finding it difficult to recruit capable leadership. Often, any action or decision will bring down on the board or committee the ire of some portion of the community. Many such leaders ask, "Have we made the price of leadership so high that community organizations will have to settle for second-rate leadership and board and committee membership?"

Another question increasingly being asked, and which this chapter will make no effort to attempt to answer, is "With the amount of monies involved, the highly complex technology, the required sophistication of policies and decisions, and the increased threat of legal liability, has the work of many private and nonprofit organizations simply gone beyond the capacity of average citizens and laypeople to cope with in their planning and decision making?"

The work done by voluntary and nonprofit organizations as opposed to the private sector has special differences which directly affect the functioning of their boards and committees. One major difference is that the voluntary and nonprofit organizations often consider their members a more direct part of their organization than the private sector considers its customers. If the organization is completely voluntary (without paid leadership or staff), the differences become quite sharp and clear. Something like 25 differences can be identified. Figure 14.1 illustrates a few.

Figure 14.1 Differences between work and voluntary organizations.

Item	Work Organization	Voluntary Organization
Leader remuneration	Leader paid	Leader not paid
Follower remuneration	Subordinates paid to follow leader	Followers not paid to follow leader
Objectives	Set above in hierarchy	Set by followers
Tenure	Until retirement	Often, "How do I get out?"
Penalties that can be assessed if followers do not follow leadership	Very severe—and financial	Relatively mild—and rarely financial
Skills	High specialist in very narrow field	Generalist
Charisma of leader	Relatively unimportant	Often very important
Leadership style	Tell-Sell	Consult-Persuade
Profit	High consideration	Less consideration
Commitment to organization goals.	Often low to medium	Usually very high

It is apparent that the director and employees work in an entirely different milieu in the voluntary and nonprofit organization. This fact has a number of implications for the work of the boards, committees, and staff.

A second consideration revolves around the whole issue of staff and volunteers. Sometimes a great deal of the work is done by volunteers and they are supervised by paid staff. This can create a number of problems and issues and areas of sensitivity. Too often, both parties try to downplay the differences and insist "We are one staff—there are no differences." This is quite unrealistic. There are many differences between a volunteer and a paid staff member—not the least of which is that the volunteers are not dependent upon the work of the organization for their livelihood. Rather than deny that any differences exist, it is much healthier to identify and recognize the differences, and then to ask "How can the unique differences be utilized in accomplishing our objectives?"

Still a third issue revolves around the relationship of the paid executive to the board and committees. It is recognized that this varies considerably from organization to organization. However, because of the factors identified earlier in this chapter, many paid executives have come to look upon boards and committees as a necessary nuisance. Much of the time of many paid executives is directed at devising strategies to "get around" the board or committee. Because of the firm place boards and committees have in our private and nonprofit organization, culture, and tradition, they receive a great deal of lip service and recognition. In actual practice they are often seen as something to be tolerated—a cross to be borne—but actually unnecessary.

One of the practical problems often occurs when the board makes a policy or decision that actually reflects its thinking and that of the community. However, the paid executive, as a very highly qualified professional, often may feel the decision is neither professional nor contemporary. Since the paid executive meets periodically with other professionals and with professional associates, if the board's decision and consequent implementation becomes known to his or her peers, it will be an embarrasment to the executive. Hence, much of the work of many executives is getting the board and committees to "buy" decisions and policies that will make the paid executive look good in the eyes of his or her peers, but may not reflect the desires of the board, membership, or community.

Another issue directly involved here is "How can the paid executive be supervised by the board, and at the same time be looked upon as the technical adviser and consultant to the board?" This issue creates some pangs of conscience for many paid directors. A related question often arises at this point, "Should the paid executive sit in on all committee and board meetings?"

What many are saying (paid directors and board and committee members) is that perhaps the way boards and committees are structured once made sense—in a more simple world. Perhaps we now need to rethink the composition of such boards and committees and to rethink what should be their roles and functions.

Perhaps some guides that may be helpful in resolving these questions comes from group discussions after management training participants have completed playing games such as the so-called NASA game. In these games the participants have the opportunity of making a number of decisions alone. They then make the same decisions, only this time they work in groups of 5-7 and the decisions must be arrived at by group concensus.

The groups are then asked to compare the results, and to answer two questions:

1. "When should the manager consider making a decision alone?"
2. "When should the manager consider involving a group to help make the decision?"

Consider making the decision alone when:

1. There is an emergency;
2. The manager has all the data;
3. The decision is routine;
4. The consequences of the decision to the decision maker are very high;
5. All parts of the organization are affected by the decision (but do consult with others);
6. The manager needs to unify many aspects;
7. The decision is clearly one the manager is held accountable for making.

Consider involving a group in making the decision when:

1. The manager does not have all the information;
2. Idea generation is needed;
3. The decision directly affects the person or his/her job (obviously there will be exceptions);
4. Employees expect to be involved;
5. Employees should be trained to make decisions;
6. Acceptance of the decision is critical.

Almost every group will identify a phenomena that seems to be nationwide. Groups are often involved in decision making and planning for what are often borderline ethical misuses:

1. When the manager is not a high risk-taker, it is often the case of "If I'm going to go down, then I'm not going alone."
2. When the paid executive wants to play the game of "I want them to think it is their idea."
3. When the paid executive wants to avoid making a distasteful decision.
4. When the paid executive wants to play for time, i.e., refer it to a group—they will still be trying to reach a decision after the need for the decision is long past.

Most indicate these are not normally legitimate reasons, except on rare occasions, for involving a group in decision making. Almost all concur that they, and others, use them far too frequently.

To assist committees, boards, and the paid executive to address these questions and issues, and hopefully to find workable answers for the specific organization, several instruments are now presented that can be used for this purpose. Before using any of the instruments, it would be well if the board, committee, and executive director would consider a very basic question, "What is the purpose/role/function of this committee? Of the board? Of the paid executive?" This seems like a very basic and almost too obvious a question. On the contrary, the majority of committees and boards have never really been told and are constantly plagued with the query, "What in the world are we supposed to be doing?"

It would be most helpful if every board and committee were to answer succinctly the questions, "What is the purpose of our meeting?" "Why was this group formed?" "What is expected of us?"

Most often, a group will meet for one or more of the following purposes:

1. Giving of information by one member to the group
2. Exchanging information
3. Fact-finding
4. Advising or consulting
5. Identifying a problem
6. Planning

7. Making decisions
8. Generating ideas
9. Legislating or conducting business
10. Socializing
11. Coordinating efforts
12. Sharing a risk
13. Performing some organizational job (become one more "hand")
14. Acting as hatchetpersons for some disagreeable task

There are undoubtedly other purposes for a group meeting, but this list covers the most common. However, no organization should accept the listing as exhaustive. Each organization needs to look at the work of its board and committees and determine whether any purposes exist that are not covered in the list. For example, some boards actually prepare the budget for the organization; some committees are responsible for writing off bad debts beyond a given dollar amount. While these functions can be included under "Decision Making" or "Planning," it is usually quite advantageous to identify specific major functions for the board or committee. The specific item can be placed under the proper heading, much as "Decision Making" or "Planning."

As a procedure, it would be quite desirable if the board, committees, and paid director would individually complete the instrument (Figure 14.1, 14.2, or 14.3) that primarily relates to them and also complete the other two instruments. Then, at a meeting, responses of all board members would be made public and the board would work until it composed a list of functions and roles agreed upon by the entire board. Committees would follow the same procedure, as would the paid director.

Then, the finally recommended lists would be compared with each other. For example, the board would receive the list from the paid director and the lists from each committee.

Finally, in a work session the board, chairperson of each committee, and the paid director would sit down and reconcile all the data and compile a formal statement of the major roles and functions of the board, the committees, and the paid director.

Such a procedure is time-consuming and quite involving, so if such a procedure is not possible, some simpler, modified procedure can be adopted. For example, the data could be collected and the board and the paid director could analyze the data and come up with a statement of the major roles and functions of the board, committees, and the paid director.

The machinery and mechanics are not too critical. What is critical is that the governing body give some thought to the roles and functions and make them public. Such a statement all too often is not made publicly within the organization.

The instruments that follow (Figures 14.2, 14.3, and 14.4) are in-depth instruments. If it is not realistic initially to involve the board and committees in such depth thinking, the meeting planner can use parts of each, or all, instruments that seem appropriate.

Many boards and committees are faced with the necessity of finding more innovative and effective methods to be used by their organization in the accomplishment of their missions and goals. Similarly, many problems confronting the organization will demand nontraditional decisions, plans, policies, and operations. Unfortunately, most boards, committees, and paid directors are too often locked in to traditional responses, decisions, and actions. Few nonprofit and voluntary organizations use any of the several existing techniques in their search for more innovative organizational responses. Specifically, it would undoubtedly pay off significantly if these organizations would experiment with such techniques as:

1. Brainstorming
2. Synectics
3. Delphi technique
4. Value analysis/value engineering
5. Innovative adaptation

Finally, it may be quite useful for boards, committees, and the leaders of these groups to consider the things board and committee members most frequently mention when they are asked to identify board and committee meetings they enjoy attending and why they enjoy the meetings:

1. They were selected because of their interest in the organization or the work of the group.
2. They were oriented to their job.

3. They were clear as to their role and function—and the roles and functions of other groups or persons with whom they were to relate.

4. The group had an effective, knowledgeable leader.

5. The group had good group-maintenance skills and were concerned with each other as humans and individuals.

6. The group managed its responsibilities effectively with regard to the time available—started and stopped on time; meetings and times known well in advance; an appropriate amount of time devoted to significant items and vice versa for insignificant items.

7. The agenda was sent in advance so members knew what was to be discussed.

8. If desirable and indicated, advance materials were sent to members, and members assumed the responsibility of reading the materials in advance.

9. Accurate record was kept of decisions reached and other significant conclusions.

10. Minutes were sent out in advance so time would not be taken for this purpose at the meeting—and members read them in advance.

11. On intricate or complex problems, use was made of subgroups.

12. Trivia was not dealt with—or kept to absolute minimum.

13. The group periodically examined its "group process" to see how it could improve its functioning.

14. Most hidden agendas were surfaced and dealt with openly.

15. Members felt they were rewarded for serving—the reward most frequently mentioned was "I really felt I was needed and contributed something worthwhile. My expertise was used. I would have been missed had I not been there."

16. Problems or disagreements or personality clashes of two people were not dealt with in the meeting; they were resolved outside the meeting.

17. The leader and the group were good about follow-up. When a decision was made, responsibility was assigned for the what, when, where, how, and whom.

18. Lastly, the group, especially committees, found that their recommendations were often accepted and implemented. They had not worked on phantom tasks.

Figure 14.2. Board functions and roles.

Instructions: Below is a composite listing of functions performed by boards. You are asked to indicate those functions/roles you think are appropriate for your board. You are also asked to check any you think are not appropriate and to indicate why not. Finally, you are asked to add any additional functions or roles you think your board should perform but are not listed.

Board Function/Role	Appro-priate	Not appro-priate	If not appropriate, why?
1. Set policy			
2. Make major administrative decisions			
3. Authorize capital expenditures			
4. Write off bad ventures, debts			
5. Review/evaluate performance of paid director			
6. Police the ethics and morality of the organization			
7. Determine the need for the organization			
8. Determine "What business are we in?"			
9. Determine new programs and curtailment of old ones			
10. Review and approve budget			
11. Protect, internally, against vested interests and empire building			
12. Appoint committees and prescribe their function			
13. Act as a political lobbyist for desired legislation			
14. Keep informed so it can make knowledgeable decisions			
15. Provide for good public image			
16. Do long-range planning			
17. Approve all outside contracts			
18. Meet as required in the bylaws			

Board Function/Role	Appro-priate	Not appro-priate	If not appropriate, why?
19. Keep accurate records of its meetings			
20. Assure that organization is conforming with requirements of higher authority			
21. See that regular fiscal/management audits are made			
22. Assure that administrative practices are adequately safeguarding the interests of funders			
23.			
24.			

Techniques for improving the efficiency of board meetings and board functions.

Instructions: You are asked to reflect on various boards on which you have served or with which you have been directly related.
1. What techniques/organization were used to improve the efficiency/effectiveness of the board itself?

2. What techniques/organization were used to improve the efficiency/effectiveness of the board between board meetings?

Figure 14.3. Functions/roles of chief paid director.

Instructions: Below is a composite listing of functions/roles performed by paid directors. You are asked to indicate those functions/roles you think are proper for the paid chief director of your organization. You are also asked to check any you think are not appropriate and to indicate why not. Finally, you are asked to add any additional functions/roles you think the paid director should perform but are not listed.

Chief Paid Executive Function/Role	Appro-priate	Not appro-priate	If not appropriate, why
1. Teach/counsel the board			
2. Administer/carry out board policies			

Chief Paid Executive Function/Role	Appro-priate	Not appro-priate	If not appropriate, why?
3. Orient new board members to their job			
4. Provide board with feedback as to how their policies, decisions, and plans are working			
5. Provide board with full, complete information and alternative courses of action for major policies and decisions			
6. Provide research and study for board			
7. Manage the organization, but not the board			
8. Serve on all board committees as nonvoting member			
9. Report to board on significant changes in operational matters			
10. Do the initial budget formulation			
11. May recommend needed policies or programs or the curtailment of existing programs			
12. Be responsible for all staff problems and matters			
13. Be responsible for all administrative matters			
14. Keep board informed on pending legislation and its possible effects on organization			
15. Advise board of new technology and its implications for the organization			
16. Provide stenographic and other support for the board and its committees			

Other Functions/Roles:

17.

18.

Figure 14.4. Functions/roles of board committees.

A. Check whether you think each statement is true or false:

Statement	True	False	If false, why?
1. Committees are appointed by the board and are responsible only to the board.			
2. At least one board member should be on every committee appointed.			
3. Committees may be appointed whose members are not board members.			
4. The chief paid executive should serve in a nonvoting capacity on every board committee.			
5. The board may reject or disregard any or all parts of a committee's report or recommendations.			
6. Any committee that has not met in six months should be discontinued.			
7. Members should never be appointed to committees solely to meet their status or ego needs.			

Other statements your group would like to add:

8.

9.

B. Reflect now on this committee of which you are a member:

1. What do you think is the primary role(s)/function(s) of this committee?
2. What, if any, are its secondary role(s)/function(s)?
3. What role/function, if any, has been assigned to this committee which should not have been?
4. What role/function was not assigned to this committee that should have been?

C. When should permanent standing committees be appointed?

   1. Give examples of such committees.

   2. What should be the maximum length of time a board member should serve on such committees?

   3. How large should such committees be?

D. When should ad hoc (temporary) committees be appointed?

   1. Give examples of such committees.

   2. What should be the maximum length of time such committees should exist?

   3. How large should such committees be?

15
Conducting Meetings with Other Nationals

Cross-cultural meetings have become quite prevalent in recent years. Some of the major reasons are:

1. The rapid rise of multinational organizations
2. An increasing awareness of the interrelated destinies of countries
3. An awareness by the United States that other countries are our equals in many fields
4. A desire by professionals in all nations to have a medium of communication exchange

We are using the term in a broad sense so it will include U.S. citizens conducting meetings in other countries, other countries conducting meetings in the United States, and meetings of other nationals in the United States sponsored by U.S. organizations. The reader will know the specifics for his or her own meeting, and can select those items which are applicable. Some of the items listed will appear to be very obvious. It is a truism that most meeting planners do an excellent job of anticipating the unusual and unique—but overlook the most elementary considerations.

It is impossible to be specific on many items listed, as the variations are almost endless. We can identify the item to consider but each meeting planner will have to determine whether, or how, that item affects a particular meeting.

All the rules and guidelines for conducting any effective meeting (including those contained in this book) apply to meetings with other nationals—determining training or meeting needs; having an agenda that addresses the identified meeting needs; varied methodology.

Two more cautions:

1. Many nationals are demanding that meetings held in their country be conducted in their own language.
2. The meeting planner should expect that the level of expertise and sophistication in the participants will be as high as, or higher, than that of participants in any domestic meeting.

The following check list is derived from both good and bad experiences of numerous meeting planners. The list flows fairly sequentially, but each meeting planner will need to prepare a specific check list for each specific meeting. Such a check list, if done sequentially, serves both the purpose of a reminder list and a simplified PERT program monitoring aid.

Items Related to the Mechanics of the Meeting

1. When negotiating for the meeting, learn the protocol involved. Some countries are very sensitive to this issue. Some countries expect that initial contacts and arrangements be handled by their top echelon. If this is violated, you may run into unexplainable resistances. It also puts the lesser administrative person(s) in an embarrassing position. This can work both ways—they may wish to communicate with the very top persons in your own organization. When in doubt, maintain the communication with the highest status person until you receive directions or signals to communicate directly with lesser operational persons.

2. Secure firm commitments in writing regarding all aspects of funding, and be very specific. Items to include are travel, maintenance of resource person(s), fees, materials, support equipment, meeting room, coffee/tea breaks and lunches, purchase of pamphlets or books, shipping fees, and any entertainment.

3. Check out your passport well in advance. Be sure it will be current until the end of your stay. Determine whether visas or similar documents are needed and be aware of their expiration dates. It can be a most time-consuming experience to have a visa or work permit expire before you are ready to leave the country. If fees are involved, determine if a special work permit or other document is required. When making multiple entries to the country, be sure your visa provides for reentries.

4. Determine what immunizations will be required. Since some immunizations cannot be given concurrently, the immunization process can be a time-consuming process. Determine where the immunizations can be obtained, especially if you do not live in a major city. Always find 'out exactly when immunizations expire; some are good for only a six-month period, and it may expire before you are to travel overseas, or before you are due to return.

5. Determine clearly how much you will be paid—and how. Some countries have very strict restrictions against taking money out of their country. To avoid certain country's prohibitions, be on the alert for "special arrangements." Much later, correspondence, delay, ill feelings, and lost money can be avoided by clearly understanding currency regulations.

6. Check on shipping arrangements if items are to be shipped. How will they go? What will it cost? Is it cheaper to take them with you as excess baggage? To whom will they be sent? Who will pay? What items can and cannot be taken in? If you take materials with you, be sure they are packed and wrapped to withstand heavy handling abuse. Since some customs agents seem to delight in making you open packaged materials, take some extra heavy wrapping cord for such an emergency. It is also a good idea to package the materials in such a way that if they have to be opened they can readily be repackaged. There is no more exasperating feeling than to have unpackaged materials on a customs table with no earthly way to repackage them.

7. If audio-visual equipment is to be used, check to see if it is available. If you are taking such equipment with you, check out the electric current that will be available. Also, take care that an overhead transparency projector does not get translated as an opaque projector or a slide film projector.

8. Some countries have an extreme paper shortage. If planning on chart pads and tablets, be sure they are available.

9. If translators will be used, take time to meet the translator and to work out how you will work together. This person can make or break you. Many of them have no familiarity with the jargon in your field. If possible, ask for one who has had some experience in your technical area. Let the translator tell you of any equipment peculiarities and listen as he tells you what will make his job easier. Never blame the translator when things go badly—they are human and can get back at you in many painfully embarrassing ways. Try to establish a friendly, personal work relationship. At the breaks, seek out the translator for any advice he may have for you—and listen to him.

10. Give translation of instruments or exercises a high priority. Always check the materials for idioms or slang and delete them—substituting straightforward language. If possible, get a translator who knows your technical field and can translate accurately. Then, let another national who also knows your technical field go over the instruments with you to see if they communicate accurately. This process is painstaking, but can be fully rewarded many times. Few things are more disturbing than to spend 45 minutes on an assignment, only to find the participants had been working on a wrongly focused task. For example, a term like "staff meeting" can be translated as "board meeting or board committee." Under this condition, an assignment along the lines of "How to improve staff meetings" can be drastically misinterpreted. As the group begins to report, it will take the resource person 10-12 minutes to determine that something is awry.

11. Meeting times vary considerably from country to country. Some will actually begin at 7:00 a.m. and run until 6:30 p.m. Others will take off 2-2½ hours for lunch. Others will announce an 8:00 a.m. start but have no intention of beginning before 9:30 a.m. Still others are very prompt. These

variations in starting and quitting times can throw your meeting agenda completely askew. Find out the "real" starting and stopping times–not the announced ones.

12. Allow plenty of time before the program begins to handle all the necessary mechanics, clearances, and approvals. Overseas mail can be most time-consuming, and overseas telephone calls are almost prohibitive in cost–and frequently take two to three days to complete. Too, some countries may consistently delay two to three weeks before replying to a communication.

13. Some countries require that any overseas travel be done on their national air carriers. Find out if this is true and how it will affect your proposed travel schedule. Some organizations like to buy the airline tickets and send them. Generally this is not desirable–no sponsor knows one's own travel plans and convenience as does the resource person.

14. Find out the locale's climate at the time the meeting will be conducted. Seasons in the Southern Hemisphere are reversed from those in the United States. Will it be rainy or dry? What is the elevation? Will you need a day or two to adjust to a high elevation? Never underestimate time-lag. Generally, if the time differential is over five hours, one should allow 48 hours for adapting to the time change.

15. What will be the accepted attire during the meeting? The resource person should accommodate to the local dress customs.

16. What is the custom regarding addressing each other? In some countries the use of first names is distasteful. Some prefer to be addressed by their titles.

17. In a number of meeting situations a traditional exchange of gifts will be expected. Try to learn what is customary and be prepared. Most resource persons try to find out what would be especially appreciated–a bit of discrete inquiry can save a lot of embarrassment. In international travel, many resource persons can take advantage of duty-free airport shops–not only for savings and convenience but to keep down the excess baggage charges.

18. Sometimes the resource person takes along husband or wife. This can be awkward to the meeting sponsor. Does the resource person expect to have the spouse's way paid? Will the resource person take care of the extra meals and maintenance?

Most resource persons recommend that the spouse take a low profile. The sponsor will usually be friendly and hospitable, but don't let the spouse become a worrisome drudge on the sponsor. Often the resource person and spouse want to do a lot of sightseeing and shopping. In fact, this sometimes is the major reason for having taken the assignment. The sponsor will usually be glad to respond to this need—within reason. Too often, shopping and sightseeing overshadow the program and its needs. Keep in mind what the sponsor is paying for. They are not in the travel, tour, and personal shopping business.

19. If bibliographies are to be distributed, prepare a small bibliography and be sure that the items listed are reasonably obtainable by the participants. It is even better if some of the titles listed are from the host country or other countries with whom they have a close relationship.

20. Because of the difficulty of getting supplies in another country, it is helpful to carry a small kit of meeting materials. Include masking and adhesive tape, scissors, ruler, felt pens, chalk, eraser, paper clips, rubber bands, and small stapler with extra staples. A small pair of pliers and a small screwdriver are often invaluable. An electric outlet adaptor is often essential.

21. Learn what entertainment may be planned by the sponsor and what may be expected of you. Some resource persons have found extensive entertainment plans that involved every evening and ran until 3:00 a.m. While such treatment is ego-satisfying, it does create program and meeting problems. The sponsor is often relieved to learn that you do not expect constant nurturing. Too, you will find that some time alone becomes highly prized.

22. Learn the tipping customs. Since some countries will not accept U.S. currency, it is not fair to tip airport attendants, bellboys, and waiters with U.S. currency. Secure some local currency in advance or while in the arrival airport. The sponsor can help with this.

23. For your own recreational time, ask the sponsor for information on good shopping and restaurants close to your hotel, and any transportation information you will need (for instance, how late do taxicabs operate?)

24. If the meeting is in the United States, learn whether or not the participants have any eating habits or taboos that must be

considered. This is especially important if meals are being prepared in your organization's facilities—owned or rented for the meeting. Some participants, for example, cannot eat pork; some are totally unfamiliar with our staple foods; some like a heavy cereal meal; others are great eaters of fruit. Some attention to diets can be a great group maintenance factor.

25. Do not forget business cards. Some countries exchange them as freely as handshakes. When you think you have enough, add 50 percent more.

26. Some countries seem to have more holidays than work days. Never underestimate this factor. Ask the sponsor for a list of holidays that can affect your meeting. Other countries are as apt to overlook holidays when setting a meeting as we are. From bitter experience, all overseas meeting planners agree on this item and say, "check, check, check."

27. Lastly, occasionally the sponsor will ask you to have dinner with someone or with a group external to the sponsor's organization. This can be legitimate and be good public relations for the sponsor. However, sometimes the sponsor has a hidden motive for doing this and the resource person can be in the position of being used. This can sometimes border on the unethical. When such invitations are proferred or insisted upon, try to obtain a clear understanding of the situational dynamics involved and if there is any ulterior motive to the invitation. If asked to appear on radio or television or to be interviewed, know what you are doing. Confirm in advance what the line of questioning will be. Generally most resource persons have learned to be extremely wary of such appearances.

Items Related to Conducting the Meeting

All the suggestions and guidelines in this book are equally applicable to small meetings involving foreign nationals. However, there are several guidelines that need stressing for these meetings. Obviously, not all the suggestions and cautions will be applicable in every country and in every meeting. However, the major areas that have caused many meeting planners real concern, and sometimes real embarrassment, are covered. The meeting planner will need to determine which may be applicable in the meeting being planned.

1. Be quite aware of cultural differences and values. Some methodologies and situations that would be perfectly appropriate in the United States may not be appropriate in other cultures. For example, in some countries a young person is never put in a position superior to an older person—even in a role play. Often a younger person would never critique or criticize an older person. In other countries a subordinate in a real-life situation would never exert influence over a superior — even in a simulated training experience. Review the exercises, role plays, etc., you plan to use with someone from the country concerned to determine if you are violating any cultural norms.

The first International Consulting Foundation World Work Conference dealt with some of these issues in December, 1977.

"During the second day of the conference, the work groups identified key guidelines for cross-cultural consultation. While having a working understanding of the client's language was seen as important, the most important factor was felt to be securing human acceptance from both the client and the client system. Some possible ways were identified:

1. The consultant should be aware of values which are inherent in the client culture, and thus avoid condescending behaviors.
2. The consultant should become familiar with the significant unique characteristics of the culture (history, geography, art, contributions to other cultures, customs, religion, holidays, treatment and expectations of visitors, etc.).
3. The consultant should take considerable interest in what people in the culture do.
4. The consultant should be able to greet people in their language, and know and express several key words and phrases.
5. The consultant should ask the client to indicate cultural and technical pitfalls, expectations, potential problems, etc., prior to the visit.
6. The consultant should provide time ahead of the work engagement for relating to the culture.
7. The consultant should ask clear, open questions, as opposed to closed, boxing-in questions, or overtelling, directing, giving advice, and "experting."
8. The consultant should avoid comparing the client's local situation with another situation.

9. While applying (foreign) consultant expertise, the consultant should continuously ask the client for assistance in doing so.
10. The consultant should genuinely look for things to learn from the culture that will be of value in the consultant's own culture. (He should not be reluctant to borrow things from it; there should be a cultural exchange.)
11. The consultant should develop the attitude that the client system is not "problem people" but rather "people with a problem."
12. The consultant should develop and liberally use nonverbal models to express ideas and understandings.*

While these 12 guidelines were drafted specifically for consultants, they apply equally well for small meeting planners.

2. Sometimes there will be several national groups in the same meeting. In some instances this involves countries with old, deep-seated hostilities and prejudices. The meeting planner needs to know these problems in advance and plan how to counteract their impact. Groups either will be overly nice and never deal with hostilities and prejudices or will fight over issues that have nothing to do with the meeting content. Some resource persons, in this instance, have found it helpful to have a session in which each culture shares its values as related to the subject matter. If done in a supportive climate devoid of nationalistic overtones, such a session can go a long way toward a more open meeting.

3. Understand that many countries today tend to be quite ambivalent toward U.S. technology and know-how in almost every field. Many of them have had unpleasant experiences with Americans dispensing advice and counsel. Participants are quite sophisticated, have a good deal of experience, have a body of their own research, and expect to be treated as co-equals.

4. A related problem is that of talking down to participants. This can be related to the issue immediately above. However, often it is due to the resource person working in

*International Consulting News. Vol. 2, No. 2. Winter/Spring 1978. International Consultants Foundation. 5605 Lamar Rd., Washington, D.C. 20016.

a different language and, in the process, choosing words that are too elementary to communicate accurately. One does not have to deal in three-letter words—nor does one have to employ jargon so complex and technical that one would not be understood in one's own country.

5. If materials are reported by small groups on chart paper in the participants' language, take a great deal of pain to be sure you understand what is on the chart paper. The resource person can be using one interpretation – the chart paper another. This is where a good translator can be of inestimable help.

6. Where translation services are used, most countries will tend to be quite literal about training aids and what is printed on them. They will also be quite literal about instructions. Understand this and test, and test again, to be sure the real point of group or work assignments is understood. Because of this factor, it is extremely important to check with small groups early in their work assignment to be sure they are working on the "heart" of the assignment and have not been trapped by a literal interpretation in the instructions or in the assignment. Understand that this tendency is due to communication and language difficulties, and is not due to a rigidity in the thinking of the culture or nationality concerned.

7. Along this line, it is extremely helpful to have in every small group, if possible, one person who understands your own language. This person can be invaluable to you to help you decide if the group is on target, and to relay to you any problems or clarification needs the group may have.

8. When small groups report their work, have an understanding as to what language they will use to report in and what language any written materials on the chart paper will be written in. Again, this is a situation in which the simultaneous translator can be crucial.

9. Never, never embarrass a participant or a group. If a misunderstanding occurs, the resource person must take the blame. Try to turn the data reported into some positive form. Most nationalities are extremely sensitive to this issue.

10. Once more, I would caution the resource person in the use of U.S. slang and idioms. This is a most tedious issue, but a crucial one.

11. If the meeting is being conducted in English, and it is obvious that a few participants have difficulty with English, don't plod ahead as if being understood. Raise the issue in a nonthreatening way, and see if someone well-conversant in English will agree to work with participants having difficulty.

12. It is quite desirable not to refer solely to U.S.-oriented concepts, models, researchers, magazines, books, etc. Spend some time learning some of the national resources and reference them.

For additional help for meetings involving foreign nationals, a number of organizations and periodicals is increasingly giving attention to this area. Among them are:

1. Academy of Management. Managerial Consultation Division. (Publishes *Consultants' Communique* and *Journal.*) This is an all-voluntary organization and writing addresses change. Check with a university contact. Last address was P.O. Drawer K, Mississippi State University, Mississippi State, MI 39762.

2. American Society for Training and Development, P.O. Box 5307, Madison, WI 53705 (Publishes *Training and Development Journal*).

3. *Harvard Business Review*, Soldier's Field, Boston, MA 02163.

4. International Consultants Foundation, 5605 Lamar Rd., Washington DC. 20016.

5. *Training*, 731 Hennepin Ave., Minneapolis, MN 55403.

Many Federal organizations and business and industry organizations have extensive programs and meetings for nationals. They are usually very glad to share their experiences.

Everything that is wise
  has been thought already;
we can only try
  to think it once more.

Goethe

16

Epilogue

This book has not dealt with some of the more sophisticated learning methods, techniques and research. This is true partly because most of them are much more relevant to planning for large groups and partly because the small meeting planner is interested in what is available now. For these reasons we have not discussed the experimentation with flatworms that indicates we may some day eat our learning. Nor have we dealt with the possible use of Telstar, closed circuit TV for nationwide simultaneous small meetings, shortwave radio possibilities, concensus technique like the Project Delphi, teleprompters, TV casettes, learning while asleep, telephone conferences, ship and airplane meetings, etc.

We are aware of a trend toward fewer meetings, particularly the larger meetings and conferences. To some degree this is related to cost. However, meetings no longer occupy the central role they once did in sharing new information. The expanded communications media make anything discovered immediately available to almost the total population. It is increasingly difficult to find new external phenomena that can be dealt with at a meeting. The most successful meetings seem to be those that are conducted internally where internal phenomena and data are shared. It is possible that techniques like casette tapes, closed circuit TV, and desk-side telephone conferences may even make these kinds of meetings less attractive and useful.

However, there is much to indicate that meetings will still hold a great deal of attraction to participants. Sitting in isolation, one cannot capture the feelings and dynamics that occur when people meet in face-to-face groups. A parallel can be found in sports. One can see a football game in much more comfort and in more detail sitting in front of a television screen at home. Then why do fans drive miles, park at long distances from the stadium and sit a hundred yards removed from the action? It is to capture the feelings and emotions and "oneness" of the crowd; to "tune in" on the dynamics that exist only in the stadium. Meeting participants also attend meetings to "tune in" on these psychic rewards and experiences.

Meeting planners will increasingly get away from the compulsion to schedule every moment of the meeting time with activities. They will become more learning conscious and less hour and time-frame conscious. No one can comprehend 24 speeches delivered in a 16-hour day. Even managers may come to realize that learning is a different order of human activity than performing on a job. More and more the meeting planner will be able to schedule his meeting in terms of learning dynamics. He will be able to schedule time for reading, for reflection, for internal digestion of content, for talking individually with resource persons and for taking responsibility to find some of the answers to his learning needs "on his own."

More and more attention will be given to the responsibility of the participant for his learning. The old bromide—"If the student hasn't learned, the teacher hasn't taught"—is only partially true. In the field of motivation we now believe that men are self-motivated. We may even extend this concept to learning and to meetings. We now evaluate the speakers and resource persons who appear on the program. Often their poor evaluations reflect more on the participants than on the resource person. Anyone who has ever faced, at 8:00 a.m., a group of 25 participants who have drunk heavily the night before and who got to bed at 5:30 a.m. will appreciate one dimension of this problem. Evaluations of meeting effectiveness will include participant evaluation as well as resource person evaluation.

The meeting planner must also be aware that meetings also provide an escape mechanism for the organization and for the participants. The reason participants are attending the meeting is not solely related to their burning interest in the subject matter. The appeal of seeing a new town, getting away from the job for a while, combining the meeting with a family vacation, using the meeting as an opportunity to job hunt, the chance to see old friends—all of these operate and are not necessarily bad. Similarly management uses meetings for a change of pace, as a venting device, as a means to divert attention and as a way to gain time for other operational strategies. Such uses are realities and must be understood by the meeting planner.

There is one more caution for the meeting planner. Earlier it was stated that if a human being needs information—really needs it—it is amazing to observe his high tolerance for shoddy meeting mechanics, poor choice of methodologies, woefully inadequate meeting facilities and gross lack of polished platform and speaking manners of resource persons. Unfortunately, seldom is such highly relevant information available or felt needed. The less this is so, the more we have to depend upon the mechanics and showmanship.

One can easily test this by reflecting honestly on the question, "How much do I say and write in the course of a day because I really believe what I am saying or writing—and how much do I say or write simply because I am paid to say it or to write it?" This is not to quarrel with the overabundance of words and meetings—it is simply to face a fundamental reality. One can get better balance in one's meetings by realizing it usually is not primarily the overwhelming need that participants have for the information that is to be imparted that is bringing them to the meeting, but some of the other dynamics sketched in this book.

Finally, we have not covered all the things we discussed in this book to make the conduct of effective small meetings seem complex. Rather, we hope the discussion of the myriad of dynamics and techniques involved will help the small meeting planner better recognize the fundamental and central simplicity of effective meetings. With this awareness, the book may best serve as a reference to the small meeting planner.

Appendix

The appendix contains examples of three types of evaluation sheets:

1. Session or daily evaluations (Figures A.1 through A.3),
2. Total meeting evaluations (Figures A.4 through A.13) and
3. Sample evaluation sheet completed by participant's supervisor (Figure A.14).

These samples can be used by the meeting planner to evaluate his meetings, or they can serve as guides for creating his own evaluation sheets.

Figure A.1. End-of-meeting reaction sheet.

Date_____

What did you think of this meeting? Please be frank. Your comments will help to improve our future meetings.

1. What did you like about today's meeting?

2. What did you dislike?

3. What improvements would you suggest for the next meeting?

4. On the whole, how do you rate this meeting? (check one)

  ☐ good   ☐ excellent   ☐ poor   ☐ mediocre   ☐ all right

You do not need to sign your name.

Figure A.2. Post-meeting reaction sheet.

1. How satisfactory was this meeting?

1	2	3	4	5
Excellent	Very good	Fair	Poor	Very poor

2. Did the group work in a cooperative, organized way?

1	2	3	4	5
Definitely yes	Some cooperation	Superficially cooperative	Pretty much disorganized	Definitely no

3. Did we freely express our real problems and feelings?

1	2	3	4	5
Completely free	A good deal of freedom	Some freedom some caution	Generally cautious	Held back most important things

4. It helped the group when _____

_____

5. The group was blocked by _____

_____

6. It helped me when _____

_____

7. I felt blocked by _____

_____

8. If the group had difficulty today, it was probably because _____

_____

9. At out next meeting I think the group will _____

_____

10. Write comments or suggestions on the back of this page.

Figure A.3. Daily evaluation questionnaire.

Daily Evaluation Questionnaire: For each question, circle the number that best describes your opinion. Make any comments you wish in the space provided.

1. The relevance of the content of the session (or readings) to your work; its potential usefulness.

1 2 3 4 5 6 7
Very   Of high
limited   value

2. The newness of the topic or material to you.

1 2 3 4 5 6 7
Not   Very
new   new

3. The opportunity you had to participate and get involved in the session.

1 2 3 4 5 6 7
Not   Very
sufficient   sufficient

4. The effectiveness of the faculty in getting ideas across and running the sessions.

1 2 3 4 5 6 7
Limited   Highly
                   effective

5. Comments (suggested improvements in method or content, additions or deletions, problems, etc.)

_____

_____

_____

_____

_____

_____

_____

_____

_____

_____

_____

Figure A.4. Evaluation.

Please react to these questions as directly and honestly as you can. Do not sign your name.

1. As you examine your feelings and reactions to the workshop experience, which ones seem to stand out most at this point?

    A. Positive:

    B. Negative:

2. Do you have in mind right now any ways in which your own behavior on the job may be different as a result of the workshop? If yes, please describe:

Figure A.5. Check sheet for the group member.

A. Were you comfortable?
Could you hear?
Could you see?

B. Was the meeting (subject) interesting and applicable?

   ☐ Very   ☐ Moderately   ☐ Not at all

C. Would you wish to come again?   ☐ Yes   ☐ No

D. Would you have preferred more group discussion? ☐ Yes   ☐ No

E. Would you have preferred more talk from leader? ☐ Yes   ☐ No

F. Did you take as much part in the discussion as you wanted?

   ☐ Yes   ☐ No

G. Suggest ways of improving this type of meeting in the future.

   _____

   _____

H. Suggest below what you would consider pertinent subjects for future meetings.

   _____

   _____

Figure A.6. Evaluation of the conference.

1. I received the greatest help from the following sessions:

2. I would like to have had more time spent on the following sessions:

3. I would like to have had the following additional topics discussed:

4. I had sufficient opportunity to participate.
   I had insufficient opportunity to participate.

5. Additional Comments

No signature necessary

Figure A.7. Evaluation questionnaire for end of first week.

1. How do you now feel about the entire school and its various parts? How helpful has it been to you? Check one box after each item. Comment if you care to.

	extremely helpful	of consider- able help	moderately helpful	of hardly any help	no help at all
The school as a whole					
Sensitivity training					
Problem analysis					
General sessions					
Functional groups					
In-basket exercise					
Interview pairs					

2. What experiences in the school so far have been most valuable to you?

3. What experiences in the school so far have been least valuable to you?

4. Do you think some parts of the school are overemphasized? In what way? What changes would you suggest?

5. What additional training opportunities would you like to have provided?

6. How do you feel now about your participation in the conference? Check one box on the scale below.

very good	good	all right	just fair	no good at all

Figure A.8. Conference reactions.

Check (✓) the response closest to your assessment of each item. Your responses will be useful in suggesting changes which will make similar conferences a more valuable experience for you and other conferees.

	Good	Average	Poor
1. Clarity of conference objectives			
2. Sustaining focus on conference objectives			
3. Convenience of site for conference			
4. Convenience of accommodations			
5. Effectiveness of conference schedule			
6. Appropriateness of work assignments			
7. Effectiveness of recorders			
8. Quality of work group discussions			
9. Effectiveness of discussion leaders			
10. Quality of guidelines developed by your work group			
11. Relevance of work group discussions to your needs			
12. Appropriateness of time interval used for conference			
13. Appropriateness of demonstration projects discussed in your work group			
Additional Reactions:			

1. What do you believe were the most significant *strengths* of this work-shop?

2. What do you believe were the most significant *weaknesses* of this work-shop?

3. At the beginning of the workshop, the following objectives were announced. In terms of accomplishing these objectives, how do you evaluate the program?

    a. To improve quality of employee training within the organization.

    b. To seek better ways to relate training to program areas, other personnel functions as well as general administration.

    c. To learn more about recent training innovations, particularly the application of behavioral science findings to training.

    d. To provide an opportunity for personal growth for training officers by gaining a greater understanding of ourselves and how we relate to others (within an organizational setting).

    e. To develop the objectives and methodology for plans to be prepared and carried out on return to the job.

	a	b	c	d	e
Do not know					
Unsatisfactory					
Satisfactory					
Very good					
Excellent					

4. List the sessions you think were most useful and least useful:

    Most Useful   Least Useful

5. Please evaluate the following. (Use words like "helpful, adequate, inade-quate, too long, etc.")

    a. Length of workshop _____ b. Reading material _____

    c. Facilities and arrangements _____

    d. Other _____

6. In terms of over-all helpfulness to you, how do you rate the workshop? (Circle your choice.)

        Excellent   Very Good   Satisfactory   Unsatisfactory

7. Do you have other general comments or criticisms that would help in evaluating the workshop?

8. Should the organization sponsor future workshops? If so, how often:

Figure A.10. Post-conference questionnaire.

Before completing this questionnaire, please review the goals of the training conference listed below. Your frank comments will be most helpful to those who plan future conferences of this nature. *You do not need to sign your name.*

Conference Goals

(list goals as defined by the planning committee)

1. In your opinion were the conference goals (see above) achieved for the group?

Completely   Almost completely   Partially   Only small part   None at all

Comments:

2. Were your personal expectations for this training conference met?

All   Almost all   Some   A few   None

Comments:

3. What part of this conference did you find most interesting?
Comments:

4. What part of this conference did you find least interesting?
Comments:

5. Was there enough opportunity for questions and discussion?

Too much   All that was needed   Should have been more

Should have been much more

Comments:

6. Are there any aspects of the work of the organization you are still not clear about and would like discussed further?
Comments:

7. Are there any aspects of your job you are still not clear about and would like discussed further?
Comments:

8. Other comments or suggestions:

Figure A.11. Participant reaction.

We are asking your help in evaluating the effectiveness of this course by giving us your frank opinions and reactions to the following questions. As a result of your help, we hope to improve the course for future use.

Course conducted at _____ Date _____

Experience in the organization: Job in the organization _____

    ☐ more than 10 years   ☐ up to 10 years
    ☐ 10 to 20 years   ☐ no experience

1. How do I feel about this course as a whole?
    Outstanding _____   Fair _____
    Good _____   Weak _____

2. Did the course add to my knowledge of how to do an effective public relations job?

    ☐ A great amount   ☐ Some
    ☐ Not at all

3. Did the course cause me to want to change the way I work with and relate to others?

    ☐ A great amount   ☐ Some
    ☐ Not at all

4. What problems have I experienced in relations to the public on which I want additional help that have not been included here?
    List:

5. Did the course influence me in making decisions about how I will do the public relations part of my job when I return home?

    ☐ A great amount   ☐ Some
    ☐ Not at all

6. Which sessions were the most meaningful and helpful to me?

Name of session	State what you liked (method, content)
1.	
2.	
3.	

7. Which sessions did you think were least helpful?

Name of session	State what you did not like (method, content)
1.	
2.	
3.	

8. Would you please state briefly any additional ways you think this course could be improved? (Use back of page if necessary.)

DO NOT SIGN YOUR NAME

Figure A.12. Final evaluation questionnaire.

Your evaluation will be helpful in our continuing effort to improve our course. Your cooperation is highly appreciated. Some questions are repeated from the Daily Evaluation Questionnaire in order to get your final "over-all" opinion.

1. Name (if you wish) _____ 2. Sex (M)____ (F)____

3. Age: (20-25) (26-30) (31-35) (36-40) (41-45) (46-50) (51-55) (over 55)

4. Years in organization: (less than 1) (1-3) (4-9) (10-15) (over 15)

5. Levels between you and the top person in your organization:

   (0)   (1)   (2)   (3)   (4)   (5)   (more)

6. Supervisory responsibility: (none)   (minimal)   (yes)

7. Job title _____

8. Profession _____

9. The relevance or potential utility   1 2 3 4 5 6 7
   of the course to your work;   Very   Of high
   did it meet your needs?   limited   value

10. In what ways do you feel this program can be applied to your work? _____
    _____
    _____
    _____

11. What was the *most* helpful experience of this program for you? _____
    _____
    _____
    _____

12. What was the *least* helpful experience? _____
    _____
    _____

13. The newness of the topics or   1 2 3 4 5 6 7
    materials to you   Not   Very
                                      new   new

14. The effectiveness of the faculty   1 2 3 4 5 6 7
    in getting ideas across to you   Limited   Highly
                                                        effective

15. Opportunity to interact, talk   1 2 3 4 5 6 7
    and work with the faculty   Not   Highly
                                    sufficient   sufficient

16. Other comments on the faculty: _____

_____

_____

17. The opportunity you had to parti- 1 2 3 4 5 6 7
    cipate and get involved in the   Poor   Excellent
    program

18. The pace of the program, the   (not enough) (just right) (too much)
    amount of work to do

19. General arrangements: lodging,   1 2 3 4 5 6 7
    meals, facilities, etc.   Poor   Excellent

    Comment: _____

20. In what ways could the program be improved? _____

_____

_____

21. How would you evaluate the   1 2 3 4 5 6 7
    overall quality of the program? Poor   Excellent

22. The value and quality of the   1 2 3 4 5 6 7
    program?   Poor   Excellent

23. Have you had a course similar to this?   (Yes)   (No)

24. If a "follow-up" to this course were offered (a shorter course; held about
    a year later; open only to those who have participated), would you be:

    (a) Interested in attending? (Yes) (Maybe) (Probably not) (No)
    (b) Able to attend?   (Yes) (Maybe) (Probably not) (No)

    Comments: _____

_____

_____

_____

_____

There is a plan for providing participants an opportunity to state their general reactions to the school as it progresses. Eight participants will serve as interviewers. Half the participant group will be interviewed on Friday of the first week, the other half the following Wednesday. Information obtained will be compiled and a general report given to the total group. It will be used by the staff as a guide in planning.

A list of the persons selected as interviewers, together with the names of the participants whom whey will interview will be provided. Preparatory sessions for interviewers will be scheduled. Information concerning these will be provided interviewers early in the week.

Figure A.13. Evaluation and participant reaction survey.

Instruction to Interviewers: Use this sheet to record the results of your interview with one person. Be sure all questions are answered. List any significant remarks substantially as interviewee states them. It is important to avoid interviewer slanting.

Date_____

Pre-Orientation
1. Were your expectations in respect to the school prior to your arrival?   Clear_____   Unclear_____

2. To what extent has the experience thus far corresponded to your expectations?   Exactly___ Somewhat___ Not at all___

3. If your answer to No.2 is "some-what" or "not at all," tell briefly how the experience differs from your expectations.   _____

_____

Orientation
1. To what extent did the orienta-   Very Well   Fairly Well   Not at all
tion sessions help you understand:

the purposes of the school   _____   _____   _____

the purposes of aomponent
parts (ST, AT, GT sessions)   ————   ————   ————

your role as a participant   ————   ————   ————

2. Which orientation did you find
   most helpful?   Sunday general session   ————

                                              small groups   ————

                                           Tuesday session   ————

Why?   _____

                              _____

                              _____

Component Parts of Training Design

1. How well do you feel you under-   Very Well   Fairly Well   Not at all
   stand the purposes of

   general theory sessions   ————   ————   ————

   sensitivity training groups   ————   ————   ————

   action training groups   ————   ————   ————

2. Rate in order which of these have   _____
   been most helpful to you up to   _____
   this time.   _____

   Briefly state reason for your   _____
   answer.   _____

3. How well do you think they   _____
   relate to each other in respect   _____
   to general subject areas?

Additional Comments:

Figure A.14. Evaluation of conference by supervisors of participants.

REACTION SURVEY

The following subordinates, from your territory, successfully completed an administrative course at headquarters.

At your earliest convenience, would you send the training office the following observations?

1. What were your subordinates' reactions to the course?

2. What are your observations regarding the effect of this training upon the subordinates?

Your thoughtful observations will (a) assist the training office in planning effective courses and (b) help you to plan a program for the further development for the subordinates.

Thank you for your cooperation,
Training Office

Bibliography

Annett, John. *Feedback and Human Behavior: The Effects of Knowledge of Results, Incentives and Reinforcement on Learning and Performance.* Baltimore, MD: Penguin Books, 1969.

Apps, Jerold W. *Ideas for Better Church Meetings.* Minneapolis, MN: Augsburg, 1975.

Ash, Philip. "The Many Functions of Discussion." *Supervisory Management* (March 1971), pp. 21–24.

Auer, J. Jeffery, and Henry L. Ewbank. *Handbook for Discussion Leaders.* Westport, CN: Greenwood Press, 1974.

Barton, Richard F. *A Primer on Simulation and Gaming.* Englewood Cliffs, NJ: Prentice-Hall, 1970.

Bormann, Ernest G. *Discussion and Group Methods: Theory and Practice,* 2nd ed. Scranton, PA: Harper and Row, 1975.

Bormann, Ernest G., and Nancy Bormann. *Effective Committees and Groups in the Church.* Minneapolis, MN: Augsburg, 1973.

Bradford, Leland P. *Making Meetings Work.* San Diego, CA: University Associates, 1976.

Brigham, David T. "Getting the Most Out of Educational Conferences: Guidelines for Use Before, During and After Outside Conferences." *Training and Development Journal* (March 1970), pp. 42–43.

Brilhart, John K. *Effective Group Discussion,* 3rd ed. Dubuque, IA: William C. Brown, 1978.

Brown, James W., Richard B. Lewis, and Fred F. Harcleroad. *AV Instruction: Media and Methods.* New York: McGraw-Hill, 1969.

Burke, W. Warner, and Richard Beckhard, eds. *Conference Planning,* 2nd ed. San Diego, CA: University Associates, 1976.

Correll, Gene. "Training Materials Grab-Bag." *Management of Personnel Quarterly,* no. 4, Winter (1969), pp. 47–48.

Crosbie, Paul V. *Interaction in Small Groups.* Riverside, NJ: MacMillan, 1975.

Dickinson, Gary. "The Learning Abilities of Adults." *Training in Business and Industry* (May 1969), pp. 54–55, 74–76.

Doyle, Michael, and David Strauss. *How to Make Meetings Work.* New York: Playboy Press, 1977.

Dun and Bradstreet, Inc. *How to Conduct A Meeting.* New York: T.Y. Crowell, 1969.

Elms, Alan C., ed. *Role Playing, Reward, and Attitudinal Change: An Enduring Problem in Psychology.* New York: Van Nostrand Reinhold, 1969.

Fallon, Berlie J. *The Art of Followership: What Happened to the Indians?* Bloomington, IN: Phi Delta Kappa, 1974.

Finkel, Coleman. *Professional Guide to Successful Meetings.* Boston: Herman Publishing, 1976.

Flarsheim, Henry. "When You Hold A Meeting." *Supervision* (April 1969), pp. 20–21.

Ford, Leroy. *Using the Case Study in Teaching and Training.* Nashville, TN: Broadman Press, 1969.

Gannon, Martin J. "The Case Observational Method: A New Training Technique." *Training and Development Journal* (September 1970), pp. 39–41.

Gouran, Dennis S. *The Process of Group Decision-Making.* Scranton, PA: Harper and Row, 1974.

Graham-Helwig, H. *How to Take Minutes.* Brooklyn Heights, NY: Beckman Publishers, 1975.

Grote, Richard C. "Hidden Saboteurs of Group Meetings." *Personnel* (September–October 1970), pp. 42–48.

Guide to Free-Loan Training Films. Alexandria, VA: Sekina Press, 1970.

Harris, Philip R. "Guidelines in Adult Training for University Personnel: A Summary of Effective Training Methods." *Training and Development Journal* (January 1969), pp. 44–46.

Hasling, J. *Group Discussion and Decision Making.* Scranton, PA: Thomas Y. Crowell, 1975.

Herickes, Sally, ed. *The Audio-Visual Equipment Directory.* Fairfax, VA: National Audio-Visual Association, 1971.

Hills, G.S. *Managing Corporate Meetings: A Legal and Procedural Guide.* New York: Ronald Press, 1977.

Hoffman, Stephen G. *Discussion Without Disagreement.* Philadelphia, PA: Dorrance, 1973.

Hoge, Carol S. *Better Meetings: A Handbook for Trainers of Policy Councils and Other Decision-Making Groups.* Atlanta, GA: Humanics Associates, 1975.

Jaffee, Cabot L. "Diagnose Before Treating." *Training in Business and Industry* (January 1969), pp. 34–35.

Janis, Irving L. *Victims of Group Think.* Boston: Houghton-Mifflin, 1972.

Johnson, David W., and Frank P. Johnson. *Joining Together: Group Theory and Group Skills.* Englewood Cliffs, NJ: Prentice-Hall, 1975.

Johnson, Kenneth G., et al. *Nothing Never Happens: Exercises to Trigger Group Discussion and Promote Self-discovery with Selected Readings.* Riverside, NJ: Glencoe Press, 1974.

Kirkpatrick, Donald L. *How to Plan and Conduct Productive Business Meetings.* Chicago: Dartnell Corporation, 1976.

Langdorf, George W., Jr. "How to Keep Heads from Nodding." *Training in Business and Industry* (April 1970), pp. 54–56.

Lippitt, Gordon L. *Organization Renewal.* New York: Appleton-Century-Croft, 1969.

Lippitt, Gordon L., and David S. Hoopes. *Helping Across Cultures.* Washington, DC: International Consultants Foundation, 1977.

Lippitt, Gordon L., Leslie E. This, and Robert G. Bidwell, ed. *Optimizing Human Resources.* Reading, MA: Addison-Wesley, 1971.

Lippitt, Gordon L. *Organization Renewal.* New York: Appleton-Century-Croft, 1969.

Mace, Myles M., Jr., ed. "From the Boardroom." *Harvard Business Review* (March/April 1976 through May/June 1978).

Manten, A.A. *Symposia and Symposium Publications: A Guide for Organizers, Lecturers and Editors of Scientific Meetings.* New York: Elsevier-North Holland, 1976.

McGlynn, June A. *Instant Parliamentary Procedure.* Great Falls, MT: June A. McGlynn, 1976.

Menkin, Paula. *A Workbook for Training Discussion Leaders.* Bethesda, MD: Educational Resources Information Center, 1970.

Nadler, Leonard. *Developing Human Resources.* Houston, TX: Gulf Publishing, 1970.

Nadler, Leonard, and Zeace Nadler. *The Conference Book.* Houston, TX: Gulf Publishing, 1977.

Nathan, Ernest D. *Twenty Questions on Conference Leadership.* Reading, MA: Addison-Wesley, 1969.

Osinski, F.W., et al., eds. *Towards GOG and MAGOG Or?—A Critical Review of the Literature of Adult Group Discussion.* Syracuse, NY: Syracuse University Publications in Continuing Education, 1972.

Patton, Bobby R., and Kim Griffin. *Problem Solving Group Interaction.* Scranton, PA: Harper and Row, 1973.

Pfeiffer, J. William, and John E. Jones. *A Handbook of Structured Experiences for Human Relations Training.* 3 vol. Iowa City, IA: University Associates Press, vol. 1, 1969; vol. 2, 1970; vol. 3, 1971.

Phillips, Gerald M. *Communications and the Small Group.* 2nd ed. Indianapolis, IN: Bobbs-Merrill, 1973.

Place, Lucille. *Parliamentary Procedure Simplified.* New York: Frederick Fell, 1976.

Potter, David, and Martin P. Anderson. *Discussion in Small Groups.* Belmont, CA: Wadsworth Publishing, 1976.

Prince, George M. "How to Be a Better Meeting Chairman." *Harvard Business Review* (January-February 1969), pp. 98–108.

Raser, John R. *Simulation and Society: An Exploration of Scientific Gaming.* Boston: Allyn and Bacon, 1969.

Redden, Martha R., et al. *Barrier-free Meetings: A Guide for Professional Associations.* Washington, DC: American Association for the Advancement of Science, 1976.

Reith, Jack. "Meetings Cost Money—Make Them Pay Off." *Training and Development Journal* (October 1970), pp. 8–9.

Rosenfeld, Lawrence, *Now That We're All Here—Relations in Small Groups.* Columbus, OH: Charles E. Merrill Publishing, 1976.

Schindler-Rainman, Eva, and Ronald Lippitt. *Taking Your Meetings Out of the Doldrums.* San Diego, CA: University Associates, 1975.

Schul, Bill D. *How to Be an Effective Group Leader.* Chicago: Nelson-Hall, 1975.

Sigband, Norman B. "How to Meet with Success." *Nation's Business* (March 1971), pp. 76–78.

Sirny, Rudolf F. "So You're Going to Attend a Staff Meeting?" *Manage* (February 1971), pp. 59–62.

Tallmadge, G. Kasten, James W. Shearer. "Relationships among Learning Styles, Instructional Methods, and the Nature of Learning Experiences." *Journal of Educational Psychology* (June 1969), pp. 222–230.

This, Leslie E. *Organization Development: Fantasy or Reality?* Washington, DC: Project Associates, 1969.

This, Leslie E. "Results-Oriented Training Designs." *Training and Development Journal* (April 1971), pp. 8–14.

Thompson, James J. *Instructional Communication.* New York: American Book Co., 1969.

Turner, Nathan W. *Effective Leadership in Small Groups.* Valley Forge, PA: Judson Press, 1977.

Unwin, Derick, ed. *Media and Methods: Instructional Technology in Higher Education.* New York: McGraw-Hill, 1969.

U.S. Department of Commerce. *Audio-Visual Equipment and Materials: A Guide to Sources of Information and Market Trends.* Washington, DC: U.S. Government Printing Office, 1969.

U.S. Department of the Interior. *Conference and Workshop Planning: A Bibliography.* Washington, DC: 1970.

U.S. Department of the Navy. *Characteristics of Selected Training Methods and Techniques.* Washington, DC: Training and Development Division, Office of Industrial Relations, no date.

U.S. National Archives and Records Service. *U.S. Government Film: A Catalog of Motion Pictures and Filmstrips for Sale by the National Audio-visual Center.* Washington, DC, 1969.

U.S. Public Health Service. *Training Methodology.* Washington, DC: U.S. Government Printing Office, 1969. 4 vol. (Primarily a bibliography)
Vol. 1: *Background Theory and Research*
Vol. 2: *Planning and Administration*
Vol. 3: *Instructional Methods and Techniques*
Vol. 4: *Audiovisual Theory, Aids and Equipment*
Utgaard, Stuart B., and Rene V. Davis. "The Most Frequently-Used Training Techniques." *Training and Development Journal* (February 1970), pp. 40−43.
Wilson, Vivian. *Concise Planning for Training Meetings.* Princeton, NJ: Brandon-Systems Press, 1969.
Zelko, Harold P. *The Business Conference: Leadership and Participation.* New York: McGraw-Hill, 1969.
Zuckerman, David W., and Robert E. Horn. *The Guide to Simulation Games for Education and Training.* Cambridge, MA: Information Resources, 1970.

Index

A
Academy of Management, 233
Adult learning
    factors in, 48−49
American Society for Training and
    Development, 233
Application groups, 52
Audio-visual aids, 67−77, 89−90

B
Beckhard, Richard, 10
Blackboard/chart-pad secretary
    duties of, 161−162
Board functions, 217
Boards
    criteria for, 216, 221−222
    of voluntary organizations,
        209−210
Brain storming, 64
Bureau of National Affairs, 61
Buzzboard, 64
Buzz groups, 52, 60

C
Case study
    as training method, 56
Check lists, 64
Circular response, 64
Clinics, 49
Colloquy, 57

Committees
    criteria for, 216, 221−222
    functions, 220
Conferences, 49−50
Confrontation
    as training method, 57
Conpar technique, 63
Conventions, 50
Counseling and guidance, 193
Court technique
    as training method, 57

D
Debate
    as training method, 58
Decision-making aids, 216
Demonstrations
    as training method, 58
Diagnostic groups, 52
Discussion leader
    duties of, 149−153
Discussions
    techniques to expedite, 63−66
Drill and practice
    as training method, 58
Dyads, 56

E
Encounter training, 58
Essay testing, 191−192

kinds of, 49–51
objectives of, 17
for other nationals, 229–233
process elements of, 16
time of, 36–37
why held, 17
Movie forum, 64

N
Nadler, Leonard, 44, 48

O
Observation tests, 190
Observer
  duties of, 157–159
Occupational groups, 53
Off-the-record group, 53
One-question technique, 64
Oral testing, 190–191
Orientation group, 53

P
Paid director
  functions of, 218–219
Paid executive
  relation to board, 211–212
Panel
  as training method, 62
Paper and pencil testing, 188–190
Parliamentary procedure, 206–208
Participant
  categories, 46–47
  needs of, 19–21
  responsibilities, 164–170
Performance commitment, 193–194
Phillips 66 group, 53
Physical arrangements, 78–94
Physical facilities, 38
Planning/steering committee
  functions of, 21
Platform group, 54
Play
  as training method, 62

Practice session
  as training method, 62
Pre/post-testing, 184–188
Presentation specialist, 4–5
Problem solving
  as training method, 62
Problem-solving groups, 53
Process elements of meetings, 16
Projects
  as training methods, 62

Q
Quiz, 65

R
Reactor panel, 53
Read-around technique, 65
Reality-testing group, 53
Recorder
  duties of, 154–157
Registration, 85
Resource person
  duties of, 159–160
  evaluation by, 193
Role playing
  as training method, 62–63
Room-hopping, 65
Round-table group, 53, 60

S
Seating, 35–36
  protocol, 205
Seminars, 50
Sensitivity training, 63
Simulation technique, 194–195
Skill-practice group, 54
Skit, 65
Slip technique, 65
Speaker arrangements, 91–93
Special interest group, 54
Social events, 93
Staff vs. volunteers, 211
Steele, Fred I., 38
Study group, 54

Symposiums, 50
  as training method, 63

T

Table and chair constellations,
  95−114
Tables of information, 65
Training, 233
Training curriculum
  evaluation of, 179−203
Training methods, 51−66
Triads, 56
"Twelve Angry Men," 61

V

Voluntary organizations
  boards of, 209−211
  vs. staff, 211
  vs. work organizations, 211

W

War games. *See* Gaming
Warm-up techniques 142−143
Work conference, 51
Work group, 54
Work organizations, 211
Workshop, 51